Presented to:

_____

Presented by:

_____

Date:

_____

God's Little Devotional Book for Mothers

Special Gift Edition

Honor Books
Tulsa, Oklahoma

2nd Printing

God's Little Devotional Book for Mothers, Special Gift Edition
ISBN 1-56292-604-7
Copyright ©1999 by Honor Books
P.O. Box 55388
Tulsa, OK 74155

Devotions drawn from *God's Little Devotional Book for Moms,* manuscript prepared by
W. B. Freeman Concepts, Inc.

Introduction

ARE you a mom who could use a break? A little encouragement? A shot of motivation? A good laugh? From the working single mother to the busy soccer mom, all mothers need refreshment and relaxation on a regular basis.

But as a mother, you know that a moment of refreshment can be extremely hard to come by, especially with the ever-increasing demands of a society headed toward a new millennium. Moms need an incentive—something to make them stop and take a few moments for themselves, even in the middle of a busy day at the office or a full day of running here and there with no end in sight.

God's Little Devotional Book for Mothers is the perfect tool, designed to carve out a few moments of time for you—a busy mother. The engaging, eye-pleasing artwork will draw you in; while the short, encouraging stories, ranging from the serious to the sublime, will hold your attention. Because it's such a beautiful book, you can keep it on the coffee table, the office shelf, or even the front seat of a minivan!

So snuggle up in your favorite chair with your favorite beverage close at hand, and immerse yourself in this beautiful new *Special Gift Edition* of *God's Little Devotional Book for Mothers*. Let this become your favorite time of day.

Train your child in the way in which you know you should have gone yourself.

NEAR the top of one of the highest peaks in the Rocky Mountains—more than 10,000 feet above sea level—are two natural springs. They are so close together and level in height that it would be easy to divert one little stream into the other.

Yet if you followed the course of one of these currents, you would find that it travels *easterly,* and after receiving water from countless tributaries, it becomes part of the great Mississippi River and empties into the Gulf of Mexico. If you were to follow the water from the other streamlet, you would discover that it descends gradually in a *westerly* direction, finally becoming part of the wide Columbia River which empties into the Pacific Ocean. The final destinations of the two streams are more than five thousand miles apart.

These two streams, like small children, could have been channeled in another direction when they were tiny springs. But they were allowed to take a downward path of least resistance and ended up far from their origins, just as children sometimes do. The best time to train our children is while they are still close by our sides, before the roar of the river drowns out our voices.

J will instruct thee and teach thee in the way
which thou shalt go: J will guide thee with mine eye.
Psalm 32:8

As a mother, my job is to take care of the possible and trust God with the impossible.

ON vacation in the Italian Alps, two-year-old Alexandra Chalupa slept safely buckled in her car seat during the long, winding drive. When she awoke, she pleaded to be allowed to sit up front, snuggled between her parents. But her mother, Tanya, said, "No" to her protests. Moments later, their car skidded in the rain, lurched across the road, barely missing a deep gorge, and came to rest against a solid wall of rock. Tanya and her husband were bruised and shaken, but Alexandra, still firmly fastened in her car seat, was unhurt. Tanya shuddered to think what could have happened.

After the family returned home to California, Tanya launched a campaign to enact legislation requiring automobile safety seats for children under four years of age. The conviction that such a law would save lives gave her the determination for a four-year campaign, even though she had no political experience or financial support. In 1983, the Child Restraint Law went into effect in California, and by year's end, child-passenger injuries had declined by more than four hundred from the previous year.

No matter how great the challenge, use your experience to benefit your own children, those of your friends, and perhaps the world's. While you do what you can, you can trust God with the rest.

And they that know thy name will put their trust in thee: for thou, LORD, hast not forsaken them that seek thee.
ℝ Psalm 9:10 ℞

Every word and deed of a parent is a fiber woven into the character of a child that ultimately determines how that child fits into the fabric of society.

WHEN Harry and Ada Mae Day had their first child, they traveled 200 miles to El Paso for the delivery. Ada Mae brought her baby girl home to a difficult life. Their four-room adobe house had no running water and no electricity. There was no school within driving distance. One would think that with such limited resources, a little girl's intellectual future might be in question. But Harry and Ada Mae were determined to "stitch learning" into their children.

Ada Mae subscribed to metropolitan newspapers and magazines. She read to her child hour after hour. When her daughter was four years old, she began her on the Calvert method of home schooling, and she later saw that her daughter went to the best boarding schools possible. One summer, the parents took their children on a car trip to visit all the state capitols west of the Mississippi River. When young Sandra was ready for college, she went to Stanford, then on to law school . . . and eventually, she became the first woman justice to sit on the Supreme Court of the United States of America.

Every day you make an investment in the character of your child. Large or small, the deposits all add up to who your child will become. Invest wisely.

You will be judged on whether or not you are doing what Christ wants you to. So watch what you do and what you think.

James 2:12 TLB

You built no great cathedrals that centuries applaud, but with a grace exquisite your life cathedraled God.

WHEN John Todd was only six, both his parents passed away. A loving aunt sent her horse and a slave, Caesar, to fetch John. On the way home, John asked Caesar if his aunt would love him, if she would have things ready for him. Caesar replied, "Oh, yes. You fall into good hands." When John arrived, his aunt was waiting with open arms and heart. As she neared the end of a long and productive life, John wrote to her:

> Years ago I left . . . not knowing where I was to go, whether anyone cared, whether it was the end of me. The ride was long but . . . here we were in the yard and you embraced me and took me by the hand into my own room. . . . I felt safe in that room—so welcomed. Now it's your turn to go, and as one who has tried it out, I'm writing to let you know that Someone is waiting up. . . . You're expected! I know. I once saw God standing in your doorway—long ago!

Like John's aunt, a mom is not always a birth mother, and there are countless aunts, grandmothers, stepmothers, foster mothers, and adoptive moms who have nurtured and reared the offspring of others. Just as He watches over birth mothers, God gives special grace to those who choose to take on the role of motherhood.

For ye are the temple of the living God; as God hath said, I will dwell in them, and walk in them.

 2 Corinthians 6:16

Parenthood: that state of being better chaperoned than you were before marriage.

14

A COUPLE returned home after a vacation to the mountains feeling more exhausted than ever. All week long they had run up and down mountain trails, valiantly struggling to keep their four children in line and safe from danger. Their tent had afforded them no privacy, and they were exhausted from playing referee around the campfire.

The children, however, had a great time. They bubbled over with enthusiasm as they told their grandparents about all the new sights and sounds they had experienced. The grandparents took one look at the parents and said, "You need a vacation." The parents agreed, and with the grandparents volunteering to baby-sit, they headed for the beach.

While they were sunning themselves one afternoon, the wife sighed and said dreamily, "Three whole days without the kids. That must be a record."

"Right," yawned her husband. "Believe it or not, I kind of miss them. Throw some sand in my face!"

Despite the struggles involved in child-rearing, kids bring great joy and satisfaction to our lives. Taking a short vacation may not only be one of the best things you can do for yourself, but it might be the best thing you can do for your kids!

There is a right time for everything: . . . A time to laugh.
Ecclesiastes 3:1,4 TLB

If we as parents are too busy to listen to our children, how then can they understand a God Who hears?

A LITTLE boy, holding his mother's hand, skipped down to a pier on the mighty Mississippi River one afternoon. As his mother shaded her eyes and looked upriver, the boy broke away and ran to watch an old man fishing. He was soon distracted by the shrill whistle of the *River Queen* as it came paddling down river. Everyone stopped to stare at the gleaming ship, splashing spray into the sunshine.

Above the noise of the paddle wheel, the boy yelled across the water, "Let me ride! Let me ride!" The old man tried to calm him, explaining that the *River Queen* didn't just stop anywhere and give rides to little boys. The boy cried all the louder, "Let me ride!" The old man stared in amazement as the great ship pulled toward shore and lowered a gangplank to the pier. The boy, followed by his smiling mother, scampered onto the deck and jumped into the arms of a man in uniform. "I knew this ship would stop for me, Mister," he yelled back at the fisherman. "My daddy is the captain!"

Just as the little boy was confident in his relationship with his parents, so your willingness to listen assures your children of your love. It teaches them that when they go to their Heavenly Father in prayer, He will listen as well.

Let the wise listen.
Proverbs 1:5 NIV

*Never, never be too proud to say, "I'm sorry,"
to your child when you've made a mistake.*

18

IN 1962, a record company executive wrote a memo, turning down the music of the Beatles, saying, "We don't like their sound. Groups of guitars are on their way out." These and many other such "failures" are listed in a book entitled *The Incomplete Book of Failures*. Appropriately, the book itself had two missing pages when it was printed!

Not all mistakes are so well-known. One evening, while a six-year-old girl was returning the milk jug to the refrigerator, her mother dropped a keepsake china bowl, filled with mashed potatoes. It shattered! Swearing, the mother angrily threw the larger pieces into the waste can, knocking it over as well.

The next morning, the little girl dropped a glass of orange juice in the same spot. Just as she had observed her mother, the child swore and threw the broken glass in the trash. Her mother began to scold her daughter, when she realized her little girl was only mimicking her behavior. Immediately, she apologized.

Your children *will see* you make mistakes, but the important thing is that you always acknowledge your errors and apologize for your behavior. Your children will then learn to apologize for their mistakes.

Confess your faults one to another, and pray one for another.
James 5:16

A mother has, perhaps, the hardest earthly lot; and yet no mother worthy of the name ever gave herself thoroughly for her child who did not feel that, after all, she reaped what she had sown.

A MOTHER in Naples had a young son who worked long hours in a factory, all the while yearning to be a singer. When he was ten years old, he took his first voice lesson. The teacher promptly concluded, "You can't sing. You haven't any voice at all. Your voice sounds like the wind in the shutters."

The boy's mother, however, heard greatness in her son's voice. She believed in his talent and even though they were poor, she put her arms around him and said encouragingly, "My boy, I am going to make every sacrifice to pay for your voice lessons."

This mother's confidence in her son and her constant encouragement of him through the years paid off! Her boy became one of the most widely acclaimed singers in the world. The young factory worker from Naples was Enrico Caruso.

What is your child's special talent? What does your son or daughter desire to do or be? What are your child's unique gifts—mentally, physically, spiritually? What more can you do to nurture your child's gifts, even as you nurture your child?

Unearth your child's gifts and help him to cultivate them. The harvest is well worth the price of the seed!

And let us not be weary in well doing: for in due season we shall reap, if we faint not.
Galatians 6:9

*Loving a child is a circular business . . .
the more you give, the more you get,
the more you get, the more you give.*

A REPORTER once interviewed the famous contralto Marion Anderson and asked her to name the greatest moment in her life. The reporter knew she had many big moments from which to choose. He expected her to name the private concert she gave at the White House for the Roosevelts and the King and Queen of England. He thought she might name the night she received the $10,000 Bok Award as the person who had done the most for her hometown, Philadelphia, Pennsylvania.

Instead, Marion Anderson shocked him by responding, "The greatest moment in my life was the day I went home and told my mother she wouldn't have to take in washing anymore."

The observation of a parent's selfless sacrifice has a great impact on children. It teaches them to share, to sacrifice for others, and to give spontaneously from their hearts. They learn these lessons by copying someone else—usually their mother. Whatever you do or say, remember there are two little eyes and two little ears taking it all in.

Give, and it will be given to you. . . . by your standard of measure it will be measured to you in return.
~ Luke 6:38 NAS ~

A mother finds out what is meant by spitting image when she tries to feed cereal to her baby.

"WILL I *ever* forget one day as we were living in Sitka, Alaska?" writes Jacky Hertz in *The Christian Mother:*

> All I had to do while Bill worked eight hours a day on a new naval base nearby was to keep up the tiny two-room house and care for our first baby, then eleven months old. . . .
>
> One day the baby had been quiet too long. I went to the bedroom to see if all that silence was really sleep. . . . The view that met my eyes made me want to turn and run crying. . . . But I only began to laugh, and then to dissolve into hysterical giggles . . . he had soiled [his] diaper and, being wide awake, had begun to play. . . . He'd smeared the sheet, the mattress, the bars of the crib, the bottoms of his feet, between his toes, his hands, his clothes, his face, his hair. Yet from the middle of all this unholy mess his eyes were so innocent!

Sometimes you just have to laugh at the situations your children get themselves into, whether it's smearing birthday cake on their high chair or throwing your hairbrush in the toilet. As they grow up, these are the precious memories that will become part of the fabric of your family's unique tapestry.

The LORD has done great things for us, and we are filled with joy.

Psalm 126:3 NIV

If you want your child to accept your values when he reaches his teen years, then you must be worthy of his respect during his younger days.

BENJAMIN FRANKLIN came to a personal conclusion that the lighting of streets would not only add gentility to his city, but also make it safer. In seeking to interest the people of his native Philadelphia in street lighting, however, he didn't try to persuade them by *talking* about it. Instead, he hung a beautiful lantern on a long bracket outside his own front door. Then he kept the glass brightly polished and diligently lit the wick every evening just before dusk.

People wandering down the dark street saw Franklin's light a long way off. They found its glow not only friendly and beautiful, but helpful as well. Before long, other neighbors began placing similar lights in front of their own homes. Soon, the entire city was dotted with lights, and everyone awoke to the value of street lighting. The matter was taken up with interest and enthusiasm as a citywide, city-sponsored endeavor.

Just as Franklin's lantern brought guidance, safety, beauty, and comfort to his city, our actions as parents light the path for our children. Our love, guidance, kind words, and correction show our children the way to travel. Even in a darkened world, our lights can shine brightly and guide our children on the right path.

We kept working night and day . . . in order to offer ourselves as a model for you, that you might follow our example.
2 Thessalonians 3:8-9 NAS

When we set an example of honesty, our children will be honest. When we encircle them with love, they will be loving. When we practice tolerance, they will be tolerant. When we meet life with laughter and a twinkle in our eye, they will develop a sense of humor.

28

BEHAVIORAL pediatrician John Obedzinski saw two types of families in his practice. On one hand were well-educated parents who raised their children "progressively," allowing them total freedom of choice and expression. Their children were often sullen, arrogant, and totally self-absorbed. On the other hand were parents who were harsh disciplinarians who made all their children's decisions. These children were often rebellious. Obedzinski set out to study resilient, happy families that seemed to weather life's "ups and downs" with loyalty and love. In doing so, he found these seven traits to be common:

- The children know their place—a family is not a democracy and children do not have total freedom.
- The family values tradition and keeps treasured rituals, especially at holiday time.
- Family members openly admit their mistakes.
- Family members acknowledge their differences and try to accommodate them.
- Children are taught to compete against each other in ways that are fair and friendly.
- Children have chores and responsibilities.
- Family members tease one another and laugh at their own foibles, but the humor is never malicious.

These seven characteristics can help you have a well-balanced home and raise well-behaved children who are neither arrogant nor rebellious, but kind and loving.

Be thou an example of the believers, in word,
in conversation, in charity, in spirit, in faith, in purity.
1 Timothy 4:12

A happy childhood is one of the best gifts that parents have it in their power to bestow.

HIS mother, Eliza, was an intelligent woman with strong common sense. A disciplinarian, she was devoutly religious and a believer in hard work and thrift. Her strong will and deep piety gave her a remarkable serenity, which she transmitted to her son, John. A diligent and serious student, John was trained by his mother in matters of piety, neatness, and industry. Attendance at church and Sunday school was weekly.

His father, both sociable and outgoing, was full of the joy of life and loved his son. He taught John to develop his innate gift for business. William was as anxious as Eliza that all their children grow up self-reliant, honest, keen-witted, and dependable. John recalled later that both of his parents were examples of courtesy and patience. He said, "I cannot remember to have heard the voices of either Father or Mother raised in anger or complaint in speaking to any of us."

William and Eliza also instilled in their son a rich heritage of giving to church and charities, the gifts being made from their childhood earnings. In all, William and Eliza gave their son, John D. Rockefeller, a happy childhood—a gift he valued throughout his life far more than the millions of dollars he made.

Withhold not good from them to whom it is due, when it is in the power of thine hand to do it.

Proverbs 3:27

There is only one pretty child in the world,
and every mother has it.

DURING World War I, one of the most popular songs was about a rookie named Jim. The song recounts a mother telling a friend how she stood on the sidewalk and watched her son's regiment march by. Oh, how proud she was of him! But as Jim came marching by, she noticed something amiss. All the other young men were putting down their right foot when Jim was putting down his left. When all the others were going right-left, Jim was marching left-right. She concludes, as many a proud mother might:

Were you there?
And tell me did you notice?
They were all out of step but Jim!

Mothers should never live in denial about their children's mistakes or faults. Facing weaknesses, and helping a child to face them, is one of the best ways to help a child grow strong. At the same time, the Scripture tells us that "love covers a multitude of sins" (1 Peter 4:8 NAS). In truly loving a person, we are not to deny their flaws, but to say instead, "I choose to love this person in spite of their mistakes and flaws and to focus instead, on all the things that make this person beautiful, wonderful, and lovable!"

He hath made every thing beautiful in his time.

Ecclesiastes 3:11

The mother's love is like God's love; He loves us not because we are lovable, but because it is His nature to love, and because we are His children.

SARAH'S second child was born with a clubfoot, just as her first child had been. At that time, such a baby was called a "child of the devil." But that wasn't true in Sarah's thinking. When she saw that her son had a quick mind, she worked night and day as a maid to pay for his education. She taught him to keep on fighting, no matter how great the odds were against him, and she loved him with all her heart.

When young Thad was cruelly taunted as a "cripple" by his classmates, Sarah comforted and encouraged him; and with each passing year, he became more confident. Thaddeus eventually went to law school. His interest turned to those he saw as less fortunate than himself, especially black slaves.

He often paid the doctor bills of crippled boys, and he once spent $300 of his savings, intended for law books, to buy the freedom of a black man about to be sold away from his family. Over the years, Thaddeus Stevens became loved by American blacks as a hero second only to Abraham Lincoln, and he was considered the greatest defender of former slaves.

A mother's love truly can redeem a child's weakness and turn it into a strength!

Herein is love, not that we loved God, but that he loved us, and sent his Son to be the propitiation for our sins. Beloved, if God so loved us, we ought also to love one another.

1 John 4:10-11

Children spell "love"
T-I-M-E.

A FATHER called his young son while out of town on business and asked, "What would you like for me to bring you?" The two-year-old whispered, "Come-out clock." The man thought this fairly odd, but on his way to the airport, he bought a large toy clock for his son. His son happily opened the present and then returned to doing what he had done virtually nonstop since his father had walked in the door: tug at his pants leg. The man looked at his wife as if to say, *What's going on?*

At that moment, their cuckoo clock began to strike the hour, and figurines of a woodcutter and his wife popped out, chasing a little boy and girl. The little boy looked up at the clock, then beamed at his father. The mother suddenly understood. "Each time the clock has struck the hour," she explained, "I've been saying, 'It's about time for Daddy to come home.' I think he must have been waiting for you to come out of the clock and chase him around the house!" The father promptly did, to gales of laughter!

When parents give the gift of time to their children, it is one of the most precious gifts of all.

Don't be fools; be wise: make the most of every opportunity you have for doing good.
Ephesians 5:16 TLB

In practicing the art of parenthood, an ounce of example is worth a ton of preachment.

JANE GOODALL spent more than thirty years in Africa and became the world's top authority on chimpanzees. She writes about the support that helped her get started:

When I decided that the place for me was Africa, everybody said to my mother, "Why don't you tell Jane to concentrate on something attainable?" But I have a truly remarkable mother.

When I was two years old, I took a crowd of earthworms to bed to watch how they wriggled in the bedclothes. How many mothers would have said "ugh" and thrown them out the window? But mine said, "Jane, if you leave the worms here they'll be dead in the morning. They need the earth." So I quickly gathered them up and ran with them into the garden. My mother always looked at things from my point of view.

Seeing things from your child's point of view is one of the most valuable ways to interact with your child! Periodically get down on the floor and play with your child. As you do, show by example how to play, how to share, how to interact, how to cooperate or compete in a friendly manner, and how to put away toys. What you do, your child will do!

Let your light so shine before men, that they may see your good works, and glorify your Father which is in heaven.
∽ Matthew 5:16 ∾

*Children are God's apostles, day
by day sent forth to preach of
love and hope and peace.*

MANY children learn to count on their fingers, but a mother once taught her daughter to pray on her fingers.

Your thumb is nearest to your heart, so first pray for those who are closest to you. Your own needs should be included, as well as those of your family and friends.

The second finger is used for pointing. Pray for those who point you toward the truth. Pray for your teachers, mentors, pastors, and all those who inspire your faith.

The third finger is the tallest. Let it stand for the leaders in every sphere of life. Pray for those in authority—both within the body of Christ and those who hold offices in various areas of government.

The fourth finger is the weakest, as every pianist knows. Let it stand for those who are in trouble and pain—the sick or abused.

The fifth finger is the smallest. Let it stand for those who often go unnoticed, including those who suffer loneliness and deprivation.

Use this method to teach your children to pray and employ these simple and wonderful reminders in your own daily prayers. Watch your cares fade into the background as you give your needs to God and concentrate on the needs of others.

Behold, children are a gift of the LORD.
Psalm 127:3 NAS

Never lend your car to anyone to whom you have given birth.

42

AUTHOR Theresa Bloomingdale writes about driving with her teenager:

The worst "first" has to be the first time your child drives your car with you sitting beside him. I have tried to avoid this traumatic "first" by refusing to get into a car with any of my children until they have taken Driver's Education and been duly licensed. But it doesn't help, because if there is anything more nerve-racking than riding with a nervous teenager who is learning to drive, it is riding with a self-confident kid who thinks he knows everything.

Every time I get into a car beside one of my driving children, I am convinced that before we travel six blocks we shall both be killed. Thus, whenever possible, I think up an excuse to stay home. . . . I am fully aware that his chances of having an accident will not be decreased by my absence, but since I am sure that he will have an accident with or without me, I would prefer that it be without me. After all, I have nine other children to think of. (And oh, dear God, nine other children who will all be driving someday!)

Sometimes it's hard to let our children grow up. Roll the care of them over onto the Lord, and He'll wait up nights until they come home!

So don't be anxious about tomorrow. God will take care of your tomorrow too. Live one day at a time.

Matthew 6:34 TLB

A child is fed with milk and praise.

CONSIDER these "Commandments for Moms," written from a child's point of view!

1. My hands are small; please don't expect perfection whenever I make a bed, draw a picture, or throw a ball.

2. My legs are short; slow down so that I can keep up.

3. My eyes have not seen the world as yours have; let me explore it safely; don't restrict me unnecessarily.

4. Housework will always be there; I'm little only for a short time. Willingly take time to explain things to me about this wonderful world.

5. My feelings are tender; don't nag me all day long (you would not want to be nagged for your inquisitiveness).

6. Treat me as you would like to be treated.

7. I am a special gift from God; treasure me as God intended you to do—holding me accountable for my actions, giving me guidelines to live by, and disciplining me in a loving manner.

8. I need your encouragement (but not your empty praise) to grow. Go easy on the criticism; remember you can criticize the things I do without criticizing me.

9. Give me all the hugs and kisses you can, even when I think I'm too old for it. I still need your affection.

Let no corrupt communication proceed out of your mouth,
but that which is good to the use of edifying, that
it may minister grace unto the hearers.
Ephesians 4:29

*God pardons like a mother
who kisses the offense into
everlasting forgetfulness.*

AFTER picking up their three-year-old daughter after her first day of nursery school, Rosanna Smith's husband left this message for her on the voice mail system at her office: "Hi, honey. The good news is that Amanda got through her first day at school. The bad news is the principal wants to meet with us."

A second message, recorded awhile later, updated the story: "The good news is that the parents of the boy she bit aren't suing. The bad news is that he had to go to the doctor because of it, and we'll be paying the bill."

Yet a third message, recorded minutes later, added: "The good news is that once we see her teacher, the school will accept Amanda back. The bad news is that Amanda has decided to drop out." The message ended, "Have a good day!"

When our children experience difficulty in adjusting to a new situation or they're just being plain ornery, we have to keep a level head and not become defensive. All children have their difficult moments.

A mother once noted that her favorite passage in the Bible was this: "And this too shall pass." It's a good thought to keep in mind when life takes unexpected twists and turns.

Boast not thyself of to morrow; for thou knowest not what a day may bring forth.
Proverbs 27:1

*You are never so high as when
you are on your knees.*

THE great preacher Billy Sunday told the story of a minister who was making calls one day. He came to one home and when a child answered the door, he asked for her mother. She replied, "You cannot see Mother. She prays from nine to ten." The minister waited forty minutes. When the woman finally came out of her "prayer closet," her face was filled with such light and glory that the minister said he knew immediately why her home was so peaceful—a haven of strength and light—and why her elder daughter was a missionary and her two sons were in the ministry. Billy Sunday added his comment, "All hell cannot tear a boy or girl away from a praying mother."

Remember to pray these things for your child:

- Physical, emotional, and spiritual health
- An abiding sense of safety and security
- Courage to face the problems of each day
- A calm spirit to hear the voice of the Lord
- A willingness to obey
- A clear mind, both to learn and to recall
- A generous spirit toward family and friends
- Wise teachers, mentors, and counselors
- Unshakable self-worth and personal dignity
- Eternal salvation and a home in heaven one day.

Humble yourselves in the sight of the Lord, and he shall lift you up.

James 4:10

A perfect example of minority rule is a baby in the house.

JEAN KERR shares these secrets about feeding an infant in *How I Got To Be Perfect:*

Some adults who find themselves uneasy in the silence have discovered that it is helpful to intone, rhythmically, the names of the entire family: "Here's a bite for Grandma, here's a bite for Daddy." . . . If the family should be small and the dish of pabulum large, the list can be padded by adding the names of all the deliverymen. A friend of mine has worked out a variant of this for her little boy. With the first bit of food she says, "Open up the garage doors, here comes the Chevy, here comes the Cadillac," and so forth. That child took the game so seriously that eventually he would eat only foreign cars.

Any method is better than the method I used on our first baby. In those days I believed in enthusiasm and the hard sell. . . . "Ooh, yummy, yummy," I would say. "Ooh, I wish I could have some of this delicious pablum." Then, to indicate that all was on the level, I would actually eat a spoonful. Even when I didn't gag, my expression would give the whole show away. In due time that baby found out who was in charge. He was.

She is clothed with strength and dignity;
she can laugh at the days to come.
❧ Proverbs 31:25 NIV ☙

*Give your troubles to God; He will be up
all night anyway.*

WHEN Penny saw her daughter's scarlet cheeks, she became alarmed. Candi had undergone a liver transplant as an infant, and when Penny rushed Candi to the hospital, her fears were confirmed: the fever signaled a serious infection. Six-year-old Candi would need another liver transplant!

The same day, Candi's best friend, Jason, also became ill. He, too, had undergone a liver transplant. Penny and Jason's mom, Nancy, spotted each other in a hospital corridor, each unaware of the other's crisis. Then, the children's surgeon presented Penny with the toughest choice of her life. A liver had been found, and it was suitable for either child. The medical team had assigned the liver to Candi, but now the team felt Jason's need was more urgent. Was Penny willing to give up the liver intended for Candi so Jason might have it? She said, "Yes."

Jason's transplant went smoothly, but after two weeks, no liver had been found for Candi. At what seemed the last moment, a liver was located. Penny recalls, "I gave Candi's liver to Jason knowing that somehow God would provide for Candi."

Both children were saved, because Penny dared to trust God. When we trust God with our children's lives, He always provides more than we could even imagine.

He will not allow your foot to slip;
He who keeps you will not slumber.
— Psalm 121:3 NAS —

Never despair of a child. The one you weep the most for at the mercy seat may fill your heart with the sweetest joys.

A PARTIALLY deaf boy came home from school one day carrying a note from the school officials. The note suggested that the parents take the boy out of school, claiming that he was "too stupid to learn."

The boy's mother read the note and said, "My son, Tom, isn't 'too stupid to learn.' I'll teach him myself." And so she did.

When Tom died many years later, the people of the United States paid tribute to him by turning off the nation's lights for one full minute. You see, this Tom had invented the lightbulb—and not only that, but also motion pictures and the record player. In all, he had more than one thousand patents to his credit.

Just like Thomas Edison, every child is capable of learning more than he or she knows today. Every child is able to find a new avenue of creative expression.

Every child is able to receive affection and grow in love and self-esteem. Every child can experience the presence of Almighty God.

Never give up on any aspect of your child's growth and development. Your Heavenly Father, hasn't, doesn't, and won't.

He that goeth forth and weepeth, bearing precious seed,
shall doubtless come again with rejoicing.
— Psalm 126:6 —

All that I am or hope to be,
I owe to my mother.

LECH WALESA, the first freely-elected president of Poland in fifty years and the 1983 winner of the Nobel Peace Prize, credits his mother for teaching him the values that led to his success. He writes about her in his book, *Lech Walesa: A Way of Hope:*

> She is the only person from my childhood I still have a really clear recollection of. She took an interest in history and current affairs, and read a great deal. In the evenings, she would sometimes read to us. All the stories our mother told us had a moral in them: they taught one to be honest, to strive always to better oneself, to be just, and to call white "white" and black "black." Mother was very religious. My faith can be said almost to have flowed into me with my mother's milk.

The children in the Walesa home were kept on a "tight rein," he recalls. Even the youngest had jobs to do—tending geese, taking the cows out to pasture, and doing a variety of manual jobs.

Wisdom, faith, and discipline all have a mother's knee as their foundation—and what a strong foundation it can be if the mother is a woman who seeks those same qualities in her own life!

Get all the advice you can and be wise the rest of your life.
Proverbs 19:20 TLB

Mother means selfless devotion,
limitless sacrifice, and love
that passes understanding.

MANY years ago, a young mother was making her way across the hills of South Wales, carrying her tiny baby in her arms. The wintry winds were stronger than she anticipated, and her journey took much longer than planned. Eventually, she was overtaken by a blinding blizzard.

The woman never reached her destination. When the blizzard had subsided, those expecting her arrival went in search of her. After hours of searching, they finally found her body beneath a mound of snow.

As they shoveled the snow away from her frozen corpse, they were amazed to see that she had taken off her outer clothing. When they finally lifted her body away from the ground, they discovered the reason why. This brave and self-sacrificing young mother had wrapped her own cloak and scarf around her baby and then huddled over her child. When the searchers unwrapped the child, they found to their great surprise and joy that he was alive and well!

Years later, that child, David Lloyd George, became Prime Minister of Great Britain and is regarded as one of England's greatest statesmen.

We may never be called upon to sacrifice our lives for our children, but even the small sacrifices we make can have an impact upon their future.

Greater love hath no man than this, that
a man lay down his life for his friends.
❧ John 15:13 ❧

A torn jacket is soon mended, but hard words bruise the heart of a child.

A POEM first published in *The Bible Friend* speaks about the great influence that a mother has upon her children:

I took a piece of plastic clay
And idly fashioned it one day;
And as my fingers pressed it still,
It moved and yielded at my will.

I came again when days were past,
The form I gave it still it bore,
And as my fingers pressed it still,
I could change that form no more.

I took a piece of living clay,
And gently formed it day by day,
And molded with my power and art,
A young child's soft and yielding heart.

I came again when days were gone;
It was a man I looked upon,
He still that early impress bore,
And I could change it never more.

Every word and every deed leave an impression upon your child—for good or for bad. What you may see as a little thing, may from a child's perspective be of gigantic proportions. Even when you think they're not listening or paying attention, little escapes the ears and eyes of a child, and all of those little things mold and shape them into the adults they will be one day.

I am writing these things . . . in accordance with the authority which the Lord gave me, for building up and not for tearing down.
 2 Corinthians 13:10 NAS

*People who say they sleep
like a baby
usually don't have one.*

KATHY and Jim were longing for the day when their precious baby would sleep all the way through the night. Originally, they had agreed to take turns getting up when she cried. But Jim frequently gave in to the urge to prompt his wife into taking *his* turn by saying, "Honey, she's probably hungry." That, of course, was a need only a nursing mother could fulfill.

As the weeks passed, their fatigue was greatly mitigated by the considerable joy they had in watching little Anna grow and gain new skills, not the least of which was her attempt at learning to talk. Even though she knew that most babies say, "Mama," first, Kathy felt her beloved husband would be thrilled if Anna's first word was for him. So, day after day, she worked with her bright baby to teach her to say what she was sure would be a magical word to Daddy's ears.

One night, all of Kathy's diligence paid off. At 2:15 a.m., Anna awoke and cried, "Dada," at the top of her lungs. Kathy turned over and said softly to her husband, "She's calling for you, dear, and I'm sure this is something only you can handle."

A merry heart doeth good like a medicine.
~ Proverbs 17:22 ~

*Of all the rights of women,
the greatest is to be a mother.*

AFTER the famous food distributor, Henry J. Heinz, died, his will was found to contain this confession:

> I desire to set forth at the very beginning of this will, as the most important item in it, a confession of my faith in Jesus Christ as my Savior. I also desire to bear witness to the fact that throughout my life, in which there were unusual joys and sorrows, I have been wonderfully sustained by my faith in God through Jesus Christ. My consecrated mother . . . left me this legacy and to it I attribute any success I have attained.

Consider these words of another great American, Thomas Edison:

> I did not have my mother long, but she cast over me an influence, which has lasted all my life. The good effects of her early training I can never lose. If it had not been for her appreciation and her faith in me at a critical time in my experience, I should never likely have become an inventor. . . . But her firmness, her sweetness, her goodness were potent powers to keep me in the right path. My mother was the making of me.

As a mother, you have an incredible influence over your children, whether bad or good.

Her children arise up, and call her blessed;
her husband also, and he praiseth her.
Proverbs 31:28

Children miss nothing in sizing up their parents. If you are only half convinced of your beliefs, they will quickly discern that fact.

A WOMAN in a convalescent home was given a party to celebrate her one-hundredth birthday. The media had been called, a large cake ordered, and invitations sent to the residents in each room. Relatives had come from several states. Streamers and balloons had transformed the home's cafeteria into a festive hall.

As the time drew near for the party to begin, the woman's pastor moved toward her to offer his congratulations just as a reporter also moved her way. Both suddenly laughed at something the woman had said.

A guest who observed this approached the pastor at the end of the party and asked what had happened to cause such laughter. The pastor explained, "Her mind was keen and alert. When I arrived, she was completely caught up in the excitement of the birthday party. A reporter had come to interview her. And when he asked that high-spirited, one-hundred-year-old woman, 'Do you have any children?' she replied without hesitation, 'Not yet!'"

Like Sarah in the Old Testament, many women are still holding fast to their faith that one day, they will have children. Sarah was in her nineties when she finally gave Abraham his long-awaited son, Isaac! You don't have to wait that long to become a mom. Consider adopting a child and fulfill the desire of your heart.

Let us hold fast the profession of our faith without wavering.
Hebrews 10:23

An infallible way to make your child miserable is to satisfy all of his demands.

68

IN *Little Women,* Mrs. March tells this story to her daughters:

Once upon a time, there were four girls, who had enough to eat and drink and wear, a good many comforts and pleasures . . . and yet they were not contented. . . . These girls . . . made many excellent resolutions; but they . . . were constantly saying, "If we only had this," or "If we could only do that." . . . So they asked an old woman what spell they could use to make them happy, and she said, "When you feel discontented, think over your blessings, and be grateful."

They decided to try her advice, and soon were surprised to see how well off they were. One discovered that money couldn't keep shame and sorrow out of rich people's houses; another that . . . she was a great deal happier with her youth, health, and good spirits than a certain fretful, feeble old lady, who couldn't enjoy her comforts; a third that, disagreeable as it was to help get dinner, it was harder still to have to go begging for it; and the fourth, that even carnelian rings were not so valuable as good behavior.

Remember, not everything your children want is best for them. The best way to bring happiness to your children is to teach them it comes from within.

The rod and reproof give wisdom: but a child left to himself bringeth his mother to shame.

Proverbs 29:15

If evolution really works, how come mothers have only two hands?

HARRIET RUKENBROD DAY'S poem, "A Mother's Dilemma,"
says it well:

> Baby's in the cookie jar
> Sister's in the glue
> Kitty's in the birdie's cage
> And I am in a stew!
>
> Time for dad to come to lunch
> Someone's spilled the roses
> Breakfast dishes still undone
> The twins have drippy noses.
>
> Junior has the stove apart
> Dinner guests at eight
> Neighbors' kids swoop in like flies
> How can I concentrate?
>
> Telephone keeps ringing wildly
> Someone's in the hall
> Fido's chewed the rug to bits
> The preacher's come to call!
>
> Would mothers like to chuck their load?
> They couldn't stand the rap
> Easy, mild existences
> Would cause their nerves to snap!

That just about says it all!

A merry heart doeth good like a medicine.

Proverbs 17:22

*A mother understands what
a child does not say.*

AUTHOR and pastor's wife, Colleen Townsend Evans, has written:

Silence need not be awkward or embarrassing, for to be with one you love, without the need for words, is a beautiful and satisfying form of communication.

I remember times when our children used to come running to me, all of them chattering at once about the events of their day—and it was wonderful to have them share their feelings with me. But there were also the times when they came to me wanting only to be held, to have me stroke their heads and caress them into sleep. And so it is, sometimes, with us and with God our Father.

Don't force your children to talk to you. Give them the respect and "space" to remain silent. Sometimes children need to work out their own ideas and opinions before voicing them. On the other hand, when they do talk, take time to listen intently, carefully, and kindly. In so doing, your children will know that they can talk to you whenever they want or need to, and you can rest assured that their silence is not rooted in suspicion or fear of you.

Serve him with a perfect heart and with a willing mind:
for the LORD searcheth all hearts, and understandeth
all the imaginations of the thoughts.
1 Chronicles 28:9

Children are natural mimics—they act like their parents in spite of every attempt to teach them good manners.

IF a child lives with criticism
He learns to condemn;
If a child lives with hostility
He learns to fight;
If a child lives with ridicule
He learns to be shy;
If a child lives with shame
He learns to feel guilty.

BUT

If a child lives with tolerance
He learns to be patient;
If a child lives with encouragement
He learns confidence;
If a child lives with praise
He learns to appreciate;
If a child lives with fairness
He learns justice;
If a child lives with security
He learns to have faith;
If a child lives with approval
He learns to like himself;
If a child lives with acceptance and friendship
He learns to find LOVE in the world!

—Dorothy Lawe Holt

Beloved, follow not that which is evil, but that which is good.

3 John 11

*Children are a great comfort in your old age—
and they help you reach it faster, too.*

A COLLEGE freshman once wrote the following to her parents:

Dear Mom and Dad,

Just thought I'd drop you a note to clue you in on my plans. I've fallen in love with a guy named Buck. He quit high school between his sophomore and junior year to travel with his motorcycle gang. He was married at eighteen and had two sons. About a year ago, he got a divorce.

We've been going steady for two months now and plan to get married in the fall. (He thinks he should be able to find a job by then.) Until then, I've decided to move into his apartment. I think I might be pregnant.

At any rate, I dropped out of school last week. I was just bored with the whole thing. Maybe I'll finish college sometime in the future.

[And then on the next page she continued . . .]

Mom and Dad, everything I've written so far in this letter is false. None of it is true! But, Mom and Dad, it is true that I got a C in French and flunked my math test. And it is true that I'm overdrawn and need more money for my tuition payments.

Your loving daughter.

When you have children, a sense of humor is your greatest asset!

Our mouths were filled with laughter,
our tongues with songs of joy.
Psalm 126:2 NIV

*Children are likely to live up to
what you believe of them.*

MANY years ago, a young girl known as "Little Annie" was locked in the dungeon of a mental institution—the only place, said the doctors, for the hopelessly insane. At times, Annie behaved like an animal, attacking those who came close to her "cage." At other times, she sat in a daze.

An elderly nurse held hope for all God's children, and she began taking her lunch break in the dungeon, just outside Little Annie's cage. She hoped in some way to communicate love to her. One day the nurse left her dessert—a brownie—next to Annie's cage. Annie made no response, but the next day, the nurse found the brownie had been eaten. Every Thursday thereafter, she brought a brownie to Annie.

As weeks passed, doctors noticed a change in the young girl. After several months, they moved Annie upstairs. Eventually, the day came when this "hopeless case" was told she could return home. By that time, however, Annie was an adult, and she chose to stay at the institution to help others. One of those she cared for, taught, and nurtured was Helen Keller. Little Annie's full name was Anne Sullivan.

Your children become the embodiment of the love you pour into them. Pour generously!

For as he thinketh in his heart, so is he.
 Proverbs 23:7

Children are the hands by which
we take hold of heaven.

HENRY WARD BEECHER, considered by many to be one of the most effective and powerful pulpit orators in the history of the United States, not only had a reputation for having an extremely sensitive heart, but also for having a great love of the sea. Many of his sermons were laced with loving anecdotes that had a seafaring flavor.

Beecher had this to say about a mother's relationship with her child:

A babe is a mother's anchor. She cannot swing far from her moorings. And yet a true mother never lives so little in the present as when by the side of the cradle. Her thoughts follow the imagined future of her child. That babe is the boldest of pilots, and guides her fearless thoughts down through scenes of coming years. The old ark never made such voyages as the cradle daily makes.

What a wonderful image to think about a child—being on a voyage from heaven, through life, to return to heaven's port one day! What a challenge to think that our children have not come along to join us in our sail through life, but rather, we to join their voyage!

Verily I say unto you, Whosoever shall not receive the kingdom of God as a little child shall in no wise enter therein.
Luke 18:17

The people hardest to convince that they're at retirement age are children at bedtime.

THE mother of three small children, each born only two years apart, often found herself exhausted by the end of a day. Along with the children's father, she had set strict rules that after a story time, prayers, one drink of water, and a final trip to the bathroom, each child must go to bed and stay there.

One night, after a particularly trying day, all three children were finally tucked into bed. So the two parents headed to the kitchen for some milk and cookies and a little time alone together. They had just started to relax when they suddenly found themselves surrounded by three little people, all standing in silence as they watched Mom and Dad each bite into a delicious home-baked cookie. Turning to Dad, Mom asked, "Well, do we relent, or do stick with the rules?"

Before Dad could answer, their three-year-old daughter piped up, "Stick with the rules, Mom!"

Knowing that her daughter didn't really want to be sent back to bed, Mom asked, "And what exactly are those rules, dear?"

Her daughter replied without hesitation, "Share with one another."

What would you do? There are some rules on which we should never relent, but others are meant to be bent from time to time.

Correct thy son, and he shall give thee rest;
yea, he shall give delight unto thy soul.
Proverbs 29:17

Being a full-time mother is one of the highest salaried jobs in my field, since the payment is pure love.

MOTHER TERESA was perhaps the most famous "mother" in the world. As Sister Teresa in 1948, she was given permission to leave the order in which she had lived for nearly twenty years and travel to India. On her first day in Calcutta, Teresa picked up five abandoned children and brought them to her "school." Before the year ended, she had forty-one students learning about hygiene in her classroom in a public park. Shortly thereafter, a new congregation was approved. Mother Teresa quickly named it "Missionaries of Charity." Within two years, their attention had turned to the care of the dying.

Once, a beggar was picked up as he was dying in a pile of rubbish. Suffering and hunger had reduced him to a mere specter. Mother Teresa took him to the Home for the Dying and put him in bed. When she tried to wash him, she discovered his body was covered with worms. Pieces of skin came off as she washed him. For a brief moment, the man revived. In his semi-conscious state, he asked, "Why do you do it?" Mother Teresa responded, "For love."

Ask any mother why she does what she does, and you are likely to receive the same answer. Love is both a mother's work and a mother's reward.

Whatsoever a man soweth, that shall he also reap.

Galatians 6:7

Motherhood is a partnership with God.

WESLEY L. GUSTAFSON once related that when he was a boy—and as long as he was living at home as a young man—his mother would never go to bed until he was safely in the house. Even if he was traveling and didn't get home until near dawn, he would creep up the stairs to his room, only to find that the light was still on in his mother's room. Putting his head against the door of her room, he would hear her praying for him. Then, after he was in bed, she would come into his room. "Wes," she would call.

He would pretend to be asleep and would not respond. Feeling assured that her son was asleep, she would stand by the window and pray audibly, "O God, save my boy." Gustafson said about this, "I myself am quite sure that the prayers of a good mother never die."

Another mother, Susanna Wesley, spent one hour each day praying for her children—even though she had seventeen children for whom to care! Two of her sons are credited with bringing revival to England.

Perhaps the most beneficial thing you can do for your children is to pray for them diligently, faithfully, daily, and in great detail.

For this child I prayed; and the LORD hath given me my petition which I asked of him: Therefore also I have lent him to the LORD; as long as he liveth he shall be lent to the LORD.

1 Samuel 1:27-28

Children need love, especially when they do not deserve it.

HUMORIST Erma Bombeck once wrote:

Every mother has a favorite child. She cannot help it. She is only human. I have mine—the child for whom I feel a special closeness, with whom I share a love that no one else could possibly understand. My favorite child is the one who was too sick to eat ice cream at his birthday party . . . who had measles at Christmas . . . who wore leg braces to bed because he toed in . . . who had a fever in the middle of the night, the asthma attack, the child in my arms at the emergency ward.

My favorite child is the one who messed up the piano recital, misspelled committee in a spelling bee, ran the wrong way with the football, and had his bike stolen because he was careless.

My favorite child was selfish, immature, bad-tempered, and self-centered. He was vulnerable, lonely, unsure of what he was doing in this world—and quite wonderful.

All mothers have their favorite child. It is always the same one: the one who needs you at the moment. Who needs you for whatever reason—to cling to, to shout at, to hurt, to hug, to flatter, to reverse charges to, to unload on—but mostly just to be there.

Be ye therefore merciful, as your Father also is merciful.
Luke 6:36

Too much love never spoils children.
Children become spoiled when we substitute
"presents" for "presence."

IN 1971, child-care expert, Penelope Leach, had a crisis that changed her life and also many of her opinions about the needs and growth of children. Leach was well launched into a promising career as a child-development researcher when her two-year-old son, Matthew, nearly died of viral meningitis. While allowing her time to care for her sick child, Leach's employer also pressed her to return to work as quickly as possible. So as soon as Matthew was out of danger, Leach left him with a baby-sitter and returned to her job. She says, "I just took it for granted that's what I had to do."

Physically, Matthew was well, but Leach found that "you could reduce him to tears playing peekaboo. The only person he was okay with was me." So two months later, Leach quit her job and devoted herself to the "total health" of her child. Today, she looks back with embarrassment that she ever allowed her son to reach such a low point in his emotional growth. She recalls, "Quitting was tough, but it wasn't as if we were going to starve."

What did happen as a result of her quitting was that Matthew feasted on all the assurance, comfort, attention, and love he needed.

We loved you so much that we were delighted to share with you not only the gospel of God but our lives as well, because you had become so dear to us.

1 Thessalonians 2:8 NIV

*Worry is like a rocking chair:
It gives you something to do,
but doesn't get you anywhere.*

A PHILOSOPHICAL clock—one capable of deep pondering and meditation—once spent a great deal of time thinking about its future. It realized that it had to tick twice each second. *How much ticking might that be?*

The clock calculated it would tick 120 times each minute, or 7,200 times each hour. This meant it would tick 63,072,000 times every year! By this time, the clock had begun to perspire profusely. Finally, the clock calculated that in a ten-year period, it would have to tick 630,720,000 times—and at that point, it collapsed from nervous exhaustion!

An equally scientific and philosophical person has concluded that 95 percent of all that we worry about will never happen. Of the 5 percent that does come to pass, four out of five times, things turn out much better than anticipated. In the end, only 1 percent of all the bad things we think *might happen* actually does, and of this, it's rarely as bad as feared.

Mothers are notorious worriers when it comes to their children. But when God says to cast your cares on Him, He means to "forcefully throw them over." He's the only One Who can do anything about them anyway! Place your children in God's hands, and trust Him to care for their well-being.

Casting the whole of your care [all your anxieties, all your worries, all your concerns, once and for all] on Him, for He cares for you affectionately and cares about you watchfully.

1 Peter 5:7 AMP

*If you have no prayer life yourself,
it is rather a useless gesture to make
your child say his prayers every night.*

94

THE actor known as "Mr. T" gave an unusual tribute to his mother. He said that he wanted to recognize "her hands, her feet, and her knees."

He called attention to his mother's feet because they had taken her across town to do domestic work—her hands and knees were used to scrub floors and toilets. He also said:

> She used her feet to walk against my sickness when my body was ill and racked with pain. It was my mother who walked the floor with me, on her feet all night long, talking to God; then she would get down on her knees to pray some more, still holding me in her hands.

He adds,

> I guess the only payment she ever wanted was for me to grow up and carry on her teachings. . . . To share, to love, to be kind and always take God with me wherever I go. . . . She always said, "Don't be bitter, don't hate, don't hold grudges, and never forget to pray."

> It's so hard to try to describe my mother's endurance, her patience, her love. I will just say that my mother was God-sent.

Feet to walk, hands to carry, knees to bend in prayer—what a legacy for any mother to give a child!

Pray without ceasing.
1 Thessalonians 5:17

Man has his will—
but woman has her way.

DEBORAH MAJOR came face-to-face with the reality of her neighborhood's condition on the day her four-year-old son, Christopher, was attacked by a dog. The police seemed very slow to respond.

Major remembered the neighborhood as a place where people took care of one another, but in the seven years she had been away, much had changed. Crack dealers, prostitutes, and gang members now ran the streets.

For her son's sake, Deborah decided to take action. She invited her neighbors to attend a meeting to talk about their community's problems. Sixteen people showed up, and by the end of the meeting, they had a plan: They would take their concerns to city hall.

Major addressed the city council, but they took no action. When her home-grown group grew to fifty-eight home owners and four local businesses, the city finally began to listen. They increased building inspections and razed ten abandoned houses; efforts to exterminate rats increased. Neighbors began to help one another paint, patch, and clean up the area.

The mayor recently noted, "Thanks to one mother's outrage, a whole neighborhood has been swept with a new sense of pride."

One mother may not be able to win an entire battle single-handedly, but she can certainly lead the charge!

Sound the battle cry.

Jeremiah 51:27 TLB

*The trouble with cleaning
the house is it gets dirty the next day
anyway, so skip a week if you have to.
Time spent with your children is more important.*

DURING the Christmas season, a bubbly four-year-old girl became caught up in the excitement of the season, especially as she saw the number of presents under the tree slowly increasing as Christmas Day approached. Several times a day, she would pick up various gifts, examine the box closely—shaking it and looking at it from all angles—and then try to guess what was inside the package.

One evening as she picked up a box, the big red bow fell from it. In a burst of inspiration, she picked up the bow and stuck it on top of her head. With a twinkle in her eyes and a smile as bright as the star atop the Christmas tree, she twirled around and announced to her parents, "Mommy and Daddy, look at me! I'm a present!"

The little girl's words were truer than she realized. Our children are the most wonderful gifts God has ever given to us. Take time today to admire your child's talents and achievements, enjoy your child's personality, and truly delight in the fact that your child is a present from the Creator to you and your family!

Lo, children are an heritage of the LORD: and the fruit of the womb is his reward.

Psalm 127:3

I remember my mother's prayers and they have always followed me. They have clung to me all my life.

ABRAHAM LINCOLN is not the only president who has paid tribute to his mother's faith. Former President Reagan also was reverential about his mother, calling her "one of the kindliest persons I've ever known."

After a gunman attempted to assassinate him in March 1981, Reagan spoke of his mother in a letter:

> I found myself remembering that my mother's strongest belief was that all things happen for a reason. She would say we may not understand the why of such things, but if we accept them and go forward, we find, down the road a ways, there was a reason and that everything happens for the best. Her greatest gift to me was an abiding and unshakable faith in God.

There are many things that a child doesn't remember. He rarely remembers every scraped knee, every reprimand, or every home-cooked meal. What a child tends to remember are a parent's character traits and their consistent behavioral patterns. Make prayer a daily habit, and let your child overhear you praying for him on a daily basis. He may not remember each and every prayer, but he will remember you as a praying person! That example of your faith will be a beacon of hope throughout his life.

I prayed for this child, and the LORD has granted me what I asked of him.

1 Samuel 1:27 NIV

The quickest way for a parent to get a child's attention is to sit down and look comfortable.

TERESA BLOOMINGDALE offers these humorous suggestions for improving family communication:

1. Call to somebody important, preferably their grandmother. If you have tiny children who won't give you their attention, simply place a long-distance telephone to someone important, preferably their grandmother. Your toddler will immediately climb up on your lap and become all ears.

2. If you have older children who avoid you like the plague, buy yourself some expensive bath salts, run a hot tub, and settle in. Teenagers who haven't talked to you since their tenth birthday will bang on the door, demanding your immediate attention.

3. Lure your husband into the bedroom and lock the door. The entire family will immediately converge in the hallway, insisting they must talk to you.

4. Get a job in an office that discourages personal phone calls. Your kids will then call you every hour on the hour.

5. Send them away to college or let them move in to an apartment. They can then be counted on for long chats, during which they will expound at length on what wonderful parents you were, and what happened, because you certainly are spoiling their younger siblings rotten.

While these suggestions are quite humorous, there is a grain of truth. Children, no matter what age, need the availability of their mothers.

Let us see your miracles again; let our children see glorious things.
Psalm 90:16 TLB

A mother's love is patient and forgiving when all others are forsaking, and it never fails or falters, even though the heart is breaking.

ONE beautiful spring day, an angel strolled out of heaven and winged its way to earth. He wandered through fields and cities, beholding the glories of nature and the finest works of art. As sunset approached, he thought, *What momento could I take back to show my heavenly friends the beauty of earth?*

He noticed a patch of fragrant wildflowers in the field where he was standing, and he decided to pluck them to make a bouquet. Then, passing by an open door, he saw a baby smiling from her crib. He took the smile with him, too. Then, through an open window, he watched a mother pouring out her love to her precious child as she stooped to kiss him goodnight. The angel decided to take the mother's love, too.

As the angel flew through the pearly gates he noticed, to his astonishment, that the flowers in his hand had withered. The baby's smile had changed into a frown. Only the mother's love remained as he had found it. He said to those who greeted him, "Here is the only thing I found today on earth that could retain its beauty and goodness all the way to heaven—the sweetness of a mother's love!"

Love is patient, love is kind. It does not envy,
it does not boast, it is not proud. . . . Love never fails.
1 Corinthians 13:4,8 NIV

Making children part of a family team is of critical importance to the kind of adults that they will become.

IT was a long, hard road that took the Chandler children out of the cotton fields and poverty of Mississippi. All nine children have memories of a poor sharecropper's cabin, with nothing to wear and nothing to eat. But today, all nine are college graduates!

Their parents borrowed two dollars to buy a bus ticket for their son, Cleveland. He worked his way through school and became chairman of the economics department at Howard University. Luther went to the University of Omaha and became the public service employment manager for Kansas City. He helped his brother, James, get to Omaha and then to Yale for graduate work. James helped Herman, who is now a technical manager in Dallas. Donald works in Minneapolis. The children also helped themselves, picking cotton, pulling corn, stripping millet, and digging potatoes. Fortson went to Morehouse and is a Baptist minister in Colorado.

Princess has a master's degree from Indiana and is a schoolteacher. Gloria also is a teacher. Bessie has a master's degree and is the dietitian at a veterans' hospital.

In 1984, the children got together and bought a house for their parents. Nine players make a baseball team, but the nine Chandler children have made an unbeatable team in the game of life!

Behold, how good and how pleasant it is for brethren to dwell together in unity!

Psalm 133:1

There is no greater love than the love that holds on when it seems as though there's nothing left to hold on to.

WAVIE only planned to skip a day of school, but friendly strangers offered her a ride, and with each mile she traveled, the more difficult it became to turn around. Her parents, thinking she had been abducted, almost immediately began to search for her. Several times they thought they were close to finding her, only to have their hopes dashed. Still, they never quit praying for their daughter. They prayed that God would send their love to Wavie and that He would protect her. They never quit believing that each ring of the phone or each delivery of the mail might bring word that their daughter was safe and well.

One day Wavie did return. She told of writing her parents hundreds of letters—never mailed. One of her tear-stained messages did come home with her though. She had written, in part: "I love and miss you more than I could ever explain. I'm ashamed of what I've done. I pray every night that God will send you my love and take care of you so that one day I'll see all of you again."

Both Wavie and her parents continued to love, and God honored their prayers and brought them safely back together. Don't ever let go. Keep praying for your children.

Love never fails [never fades out or becomes obsolete or comes to an end].

❧ 1 Corinthians 13:8 AMP ❧

Every mother is like Moses.
She does not enter the Promised Land.
She prepares a world she will not see.

WHEN W. P. L. Mackay was seventeen, he left his humble Scottish home to attend college. His mother gave him a Bible in which she had inscribed his name and a verse of Scripture. Unfortunately, college was only the beginning of a downhill slide. At one point, he pawned the Bible to get money for whiskey. His mother continued praying for him until she died.

Eventually, Mackay became a doctor. While working in a hospital, he encountered a dying patient who repeatedly asked for his "book." After the man died, Mackay searched the hospital room to find what book had been so important to a dying man. He was surprised to find the very Bible he had once pawned!

Mackay went to his office and stared at the familiar writing of his mother. He thumbed through the pages, reading the many verses his mother had underscored in hopes her son might heed them. After many hours of reading and reflection, Mackay prayed to God for mercy. The physician later became a minister. The book he once pawned became his most precious possession.

You may not live to see how your children "turn out." But you can trust that nothing you do for their spiritual wholeness will have been in vain. God always listens to a mother's prayers!

Then the LORD said to him, "This is the land I promised on oath to Abraham, Isaac and Jacob. . . . I have let you see it with your eyes, but you will not cross over into it."
Deuteronomy 34:4 NIV

A food is not necessarily essential just because your child hates it.

IN *Family—The Ties That Bind and Gag!* Erma Bombeck writes:

In retrospect, it was only a matter of time before the Family Dinner Hour passed into history and fast foods took over. . . . My pot roast gave way to pizza. . . . My burgers couldn't compete with the changing numbers under the Golden Arches. I couldn't even do chicken right!

The old rules for eating at home—sit up straight, chew your food, and don't laugh with cottage cheese in your mouth—didn't fit the new ambiance. A new set of rules emerged.

Bombeck suggests these new rules:

When ordering from the back seat of the car, do not cup your mouth over Daddy's ear and shout.

Never order more than you can balance between your knees.

Front-of-the-car seating is better than the back seat if you have a choice. The dashboard offers space for holding beverages.

Afterward, each person should be responsible for his or her trash and should contain it in a bag. Two-week-old onion rings in the ashtray are not a pretty sight.

While we may laugh at these rules, many of us can relate. If you must dine in the car, make it a family time. If you lock all the doors and drive fast, you have a captive audience!

You have filled my heart with greater joy.

⭐ Psalm 4:7 NIV ⭐

*God sends children for a greater purpose
than merely to propagate the human race.
They are born to enlarge our hearts, make us
unselfish, and fill us full of kindly
sympathies and affections.*

IN 1981, Elizabeth Glaser gave birth to a girl, Ariel. But moments after Ari was born, Elizabeth began to hemorrhage. She remembers watching silently as she received a transfusion of seven pints of blood—contaminated by HIV. Four years later, Ariel began to suffer baffling stomach pains and draining fatigue. She underwent a battery of tests, one of which gave a name to her illness: AIDS.

After Ariel's death, Elizabeth became an AIDS activist, co-founding the Pediatric AIDS Foundation. Many consider her to be the most effective AIDS lobbyist in the nation. She says of Ariel:

> It was Ari who taught me to love when all I wanted to do was hate. She taught me to be brave when all I felt was fear. And she taught me to help others when all I wanted to do was help myself. I am active in fighting AIDS because I want to be a person she would be proud of; I was so proud of her . . . I think about her courage and I am able to go on.

About living with HIV, Elizabeth said, "Everything—from making peanut butter sandwiches and watching Jake [her son] play ball to plating the garden—has significance to me."

Children add another dimension to our lives—selflessness.

My little children, let us not love in word,
neither in tongue; but in deed and in truth.
1 John 3:18

Every mother has the breathtaking privilege of sharing with God in the creation of new life. She helps bring into existence a soul that will endure for all eternity.

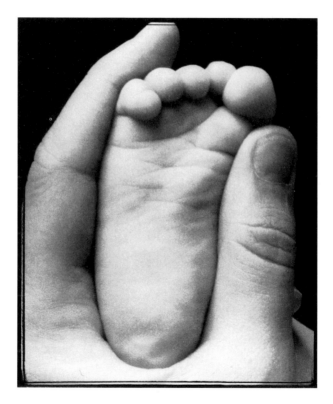

A PROFESSOR in a world-acclaimed medical school once posed this medical situation—an ethical problem—to his students:

Here's the family history: The father has syphilis. The mother has TB. They have already had four children. The first is blind. The second died. The third is deaf. The fourth has TB. Now the mother is pregnant again. The parents come to you for advice. They are willing to have an abortion, if you decide they should. What do you say?

The students gave various individual opinions, and then the professor asked them to break into small groups for "consultation." All of the groups came back to report that they would recommend abortion.

"Congratulations," the professor said, "you just took the life of Beethoven!"

A woman helps create the body of her child, and as her child grows, she nurtures his or her emotions and intellect. Only God, however, can create the child's eternal soul. A soul must have a body on this earth. A body has a soul. Both God and mother are partners in the creation of a baby from the moment of conception.

No privilege is greater than the privilege of creating another human being. And no one act requires greater faith!

For Thou didst form my inward parts;
Thou didst weave me in my mother's womb.
Psalm 139:13 NAS

We need to be patient with our children in the same way God is patient with us.

ONE of the most beautiful descriptions of patience in all of classic literature is this from Bishop Horne:

Patience is the guardian of faith, the preserver of peace, the cherisher of love, the teacher of humility. Patience governs the flesh, strengthens the spirit, sweetens the temper, stifles anger, extinguishes envy, subdues pride; she bridles the tongue, restrains the hand, tramples upon temptations, endures persecutions, consummates martyrdom.

Patience produces unity in the church, loyalty in the state, harmony in families and societies; she comforts the poor, and moderates the rich; she makes us humble in prosperity, cheerful in adversity, unmoved by calumny and reproach; she teaches us to forgive those who have injured us, and to be the first in asking forgiveness of those whom we have injured; she delights the faithful, and invites the unbelieving; she adorns the woman, and approves the man; she is beautiful in either sex and every age. . . .

She rides not in the whirlwind and stormy tempest of passion, but her throne is the humble and contrite heart, and her kingdom is the kingdom of peace.

Remember, when the opportunity arises to be patient with your child, consider how God would respond to you in a similar circumstance.

The discretion of a man deferreth his anger; and it is his glory to pass over a transgression.
Proverbs 19:11

A child is a gift whose worth cannot be measured except by the heart.

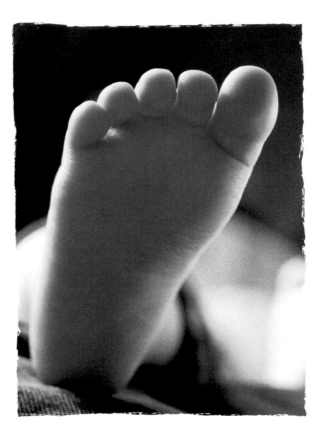

MARGARET BOURKE-WHITE, one of the innovators of the photo essay, was one of the first four staff photographers of *Life* magazine when it began in 1936. She was also the first woman photographer ever attached to the U.S. armed forces in World War II. From early years, Margaret knew that she was counted as a "gift" to her parents. She recalls her mother telling her, "Margaret, you can always be proud that you were invited into the world."

In her autobiography, aptly titled *Portrait of Myself,* she writes:

I don't know where she got this fine philosophy that children should come because they were wanted. . . . When each of her own three children was on the way, Mother would say to those closest to her, "I don't know whether this will be a boy or girl and I don't care. But this child was invited into the world and it will be a wonderful child." She was explicit about the invitation and believed the child should be the welcomed result of a known and definite act of love between man and woman.

Have you told your child today that he or she is a gift—a child you wanted and "invited" into the world? What good news that is to a child's ears!

Behold, children are a gift of the LORD;
The fruit of the womb is a reward.
❧ Psalm 127:3 NAS ❧

Expect great things from God, and attempt great things for God.

GLADYS AYLWARD saw herself as a simple woman who just did what God called her to do. Yet, her life was so remarkable that both a book, *The Small Woman,* and a movie, *The Inn of Sixth Happiness,* were produced about the great things God accomplished through her.

A British citizen, Aylward left her home in 1920 and sailed for China. There she bought orphans who were being systematically discarded, children who had been displaced by the political upheavals of the time and left to starve or wander on their own until placed in government warehouses. Gladys gave these children a home.

When the Japanese invaded China, she was forced to flee the mainland with 100 children. She ended up on the island of Formosa with her charges. There she continued to devote her life to raising children who knew no other mother.

Gladys explains her amazing work for God like this: "I did not choose this. I was led into it by God. I am not really more interested in children than I am in other people, but God through His Holy Spirit gave me to understand that this is what He wanted me to do, so I did."

Truly, truly, I say to you, he who believes in Me,
the works that I do shall he do also; and greater works
than these shall he do; because I go to the Father.
John 14:12 NAS

*Children certainly brighten up a home.
Did you ever see a child under twelve
turn off an electric light?*

PARENTS have a few habits that children never seem to understand, or to copy—such as flipping off lights in rooms with no one in them and turning off faucets in a bathroom. In *Family–The Ties That Bind and Gag!*, author Erma Bombeck offers these "Commandments for the Utilities":

1. Thou shalt flush. Especially if thou is fifteen years old and has the use of both arms.
2. Thou shalt hang up the phone when thou has been on it long enough for the rates to change.
3. Thou shalt not stand in front of the refrigerator door waiting for something to dance.
4. Thou shalt not covet the rest of the family's hot water.
5. Thou shalt honor thy father and mother's thermostat and keep it normal.
6. Thou shalt remember last month's electricity bill and rejoice in darkness.

Unfortunately, notes Bombeck, these commandments generally lay in a family like broken stone tablets amidst wet towels and melting soap!

One of the best antidotes for the stresses of motherhood is laughter. Take another look at the above rules. Chances are you can identify with the frustration that birthed them and even come up with a few of your own.

Fill all who love you with your happiness.

Psalm 5:11 TLB

Our children watch us live out our lives, and who we are shouts louder than anything we might say.

126

126

ACCORDING to an old story, there once was a mother who had an only son, to whom she gave everything as he was growing up. It made him selfish. When he grew up, he was unkind to his mother, refusing to support her, and turned her out of her own house.

As the old woman prepared to leave her home, she turned to her youngest grandson and said, "Go and fetch the covering from my bed, that I may go and sit by the wayside and wrap myself in it and beg for alms."

The child burst into tears and ran for the covering. But rather than take it to his grandmother, he ran to his father and said, "Oh father, grandmother has asked for this so she can keep herself warm as she sits by the road and begs. Please cut it into two pieces. Half of it will be large enough for grandmother. And you may want the other half when I am grown to be a man and turn you out-of-doors."

The uncaring son ran to his mother, asked her forgiveness, and took care of her until her death.

Actions speak far louder than words. How we treat our parents will be how we will be treated by our children when we are old.

In everything set them an example by doing what is good.
❧ Titus 2:7 NIV ❧

Happy is the child . . . who sees mother and father rising early, or going aside regularly, to keep times with the Lord.

PARENTS today often use dozens of excuses to justify not taking their children to church or having a family devotional time, but if that urge strikes you, remember the family of Lydia Murphy. She moved with her parents to Shawnee, Kansas, in 1859, and she writes of their first night in their new home:

The family Bible rested in the center of the room. We gathered around the table, seated on boxes and improvised chairs, while the usual evening family prayers were held after the reading of a chapter of the Scriptures. During the fifty years of his Kansas citizenship, this morning and evening Scripture reading and prayer was not once omitted in my father's house.

The Murphys had been devout Methodists, but the nearest Methodist church was ten miles away. They therefore secured the services of a circuit-riding Methodist minister and opened their own home for worship, welcoming neighbors of all denominations. Within months, their home had become the center of both the social and religious life of the community. Services were held every two weeks on Saturdays.

A child who sees his parents spend time with God has a sense of security that little else can ever establish. Pass on that tradition to your children.

Let the heart of them rejoice that seek the LORD.
Seek the LORD, and his strength: seek his face evermore.
Psalm 105:3-4

*You can do everything else right as a parent,
but if you don't begin with loving God,
you're going to fail.*

SARAH EDWARDS, wife of revivalist and theologian Jonathan Edwards, bore eleven children. At her death, Samuel Hopkins eulogized her in this way:

> She had an excellent way of governing her children. She knew how to make them regard and obey her cheerfully, without loud, angry words, much less heavy blows. . . . If any correction was necessary, she did not administer it in a passion. . . . In her directions in matters of importance, she would address herself to the reason of her children, that they might not only know her will, but at the same time be convinced of the reasonableness of it. . . . Her system of discipline was begun at a very early age and it was her rule to resist the first as well as every subsequent exhibition of temper or disobedience in the child . . . wisely reflecting that until a child will obey his parents, he can never be brought to obey God.

At the close of each day, after all in the family were in bed, Sarah and her husband shared a devotional time together in his study. With eleven children to "tuck in," Sarah did not allow any of them leeway in keeping her from this cherished time with her husband!

The LORD our God is one LORD: And thou shalt love the LORD thy God with all thine heart, and with all thy soul, and with all thy might.

Deuteronomy 6:4-5

Beautiful as seemed mama's face, it became incomparably more lovely when she smiled, and seemed to enliven everything about her.

FOR more than a century, the majestic statue titled "Liberty Enlightening the World" has towered near the entrance to New York Harbor as a symbol of America's freedom.

The famous sculptor of the statue, Bartholdi, spent twenty years supervising the construction of his masterpiece. He personally helped raise the four million dollars needed to pay for the statue, which was presented by France as a gift to the United States. When the fund-raising program for the statue lagged, Bartholdi pledged his own private fortune to keep the project funded and practically impoverished himself in the process.

At the start, when Bartholdi was seeking for a model on whom to pattern "Liberty," he received a great deal of advice from art experts. Most of the leading authorities advised him to find a grand heroic figure as his pattern. After examining countless heroes, however, Bartholdi chose as his model his own mother. Just as no other statue in the world so eloquently lights the way to freedom, so no other woman so beautifully lighted Bartholdi's own world.

Remember, your children are watching even the very expressions of your face. Be sure it wears a smile most of the time!

For the joy of the LORD is your strength.
Nehemiah 8:10

133

No one is useless in this world who lightens the burden of it for someone else.

CAROL PORTER, a registered nurse, is a co-founder of Kid-Care, Inc., a nonprofit group with a volunteer staff which delivers 500 free meals each day to poor neighborhoods. Each meal is prepared in Porter's cramped Houston home, where extra stoves and refrigerators have been installed in what used to be the family's living room and den. Kid-Care receives no public funding, and although Carol's efforts have resulted in help from some corporations, most of her $500,000 budget comes from individual donations.

Carol credits her late mother, Lula Doe, for giving her the idea for Kid-Care. In 1984, Lula persuaded a local supermarket not to discard its blemished produce but to let her distribute it to the poor.

During the 1989 Christmas season, Carol saw a group of children searching for food in a McDonald's dumpster. She says, "I saw third world conditions a stone's throw from where I live." Kid-Care was her response.

"People ask me what's in it for me. And I tell them to go the route with me and see my kids' faces. That's what's in it for me." She sees the meals as "better than ice cream. . . . It's hope."

Purpose in life comes when we determine to lift the load of another . . . to show God's love by doing for them what they could not do for themselves. Kids are a great place to start!

Bear ye one another's burdens, and so fulfil the law of Christ.
Galatians 6:2

Cleaning your house while your kids are still growing is like shoveling the walk before it stops snowing.

ELINOR GOULDING SMITH offers this analysis of a child's room:

The child's room is a sight to make strong men faint, and induces in mothers a condition characterized by trembling, pallor, dysphasia, [and] weakness. . . .

The room is characterized by litter to a depth of two to three feet, except under the bed where it is perhaps only six inches deep. You can see no article of furniture, each being buried completely, and emerging as simply a higher mound of rubbish.

A few bits of furniture stick up above the level of the rubbish—the very top of a desk lamp protrudes above a mountain of papers, books, crayons, hedge shears, gym sneakers, the remains of a tongue sandwich, two peach pits, a camera, a microscope, some jars of extremely aromatic pond water, a deck of marked cards, coping saw, overdue library books, bicycle tire pumps, a Siamese fighting fish no longer in the prime of life who lives in the bottom half of a cider jug, and so on . . . right up to the top of the desk lamp. You look at the top of the lamp happily. "At last," you say as you totter across the room, "a landmark!"

Relax. Your kids are only young once, and the time goes by much too quickly.

A merry heart doeth good like a medicine.
◁ Proverbs 17:22 ▷

Nothing has a better effect upon children than praise.

A MOTHER once left her children with her single sister in order to work overseas for three weeks. Although she missed her children tremendously, she was also glad for a break. As a single parent, she was feeling worn out, struggling to juggle her job and her role as a mother. The demands of constant discipline sometimes seemed too much. As she prepared to return home, she thought, *I wonder how Sis coped. I hope she heeded my warning not to let them get away with murder.*

To her surprise, she arrived at her sister's home to find her children playing quietly, eager to see her but quick to obey her sister's slightest request. "What did you do?" she whispered to her sister. "They're never this well behaved!" Her sister replied, "Nothing, really. Before you left, I read a little article about parenting and I just did what it said." The woman said, "What was it? Give me the formula!"

The sister picked up the article and read, "Tell children what to do, far more than you tell them what not to do. And then praise them for what they do—instead of criticizing them for what they don't do." Smiling at her sister, she added, "It seemed to work!"

Anxiety in the heart of a man weighs it down,
but a good word makes it glad.

Proverbs 12:25 NAS

*A house without love may be a castle, or
a palace, but it is not a home;
love is the life of a true home.*

WOMEN are often tempted to think that their homemaking skills are what turn a house into a home. But consider how one of the most famous cooks of all time, Julia Child, recalls her own childhood:

> I know I'm happy. I was very fortunate in my family background because I had a very loving, supportive family. We had no conflict. My sister was five years younger, and we had a brother halfway between, so we never had any sibling rivalry. My parents were happy; we were not rich, but comfortably well-off. My mother thought everything we did was absolutely marvelous. I think your background makes an awful lot of difference. I don't know what you do if you've been abused, or haven't been praised enough so that you don't feel that you're okay. I was very fortunate in having such a happy background. I was never brilliant in school, but I never had any problems either, so I didn't feel inferior. I did have the problem of being twice as tall as anyone else, but that didn't seem to make any difference because my mother always said we were so wonderful, no matter what.

Notice Julia didn't make one mention of her mother's cooking skills or food, only of her praise! One word of praise from your mother is worth ten from someone else.

Better a dry crust with peace and quiet
than a house full of feasting, with strife.
— Proverbs 17:1 NIV —

*The more a child becomes aware of
a mother's willingness to listen,
the more a mother will begin to hear.*

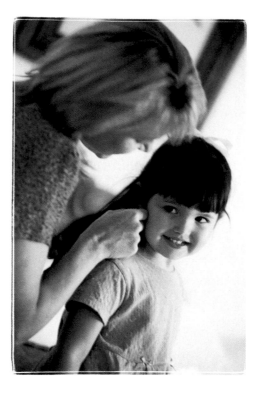

A BUSY mother of four children found her job as wife and mom a careful balancing act. She had found the most efficient way to handle the weekly grocery shopping was to go alone, unhampered by "help" that usually inflated her grocery bill and strained her patience.

On one shopping day, her thirteen-year-old son asked, "Where ya goin', Mom?" She replied, "To the grocery store. I'll be back soon." Her son asked, "Can I go with you?" She almost had the words "Some other time" out of her mouth when something inside made her say, "Okay."

Once in the car, she braced herself for the struggle she anticipated over the radio. Instead, her son began to talk. "When I grow up, I'm going to be rich," he announced. "Oh?" she said.

"Yeah," he said. "Then I can give my kids everything they want." She asked, "Do you know any kid who gets everything he wants?" Her son gave her the name of such a child. "Do you like him?" Mom asked. After a long pause, he grinned and said, "Naw, he's the meanest, most unhappy kid I know. His dad's never around and his mom's always too busy."

When the opportunity presents itself, make yourself available to your kids. It's worth the effort.

A wise man will hear, and will increase learning; and a man of understanding shall attain unto wise counsels.

Proverbs 1:5

*Anytime a child can be seen but not heard,
it's a shame to wake him.*

144

A SALESMAN telephoned a household, and a four-year-old boy answered. He said, "May I speak to your mother, please?"

The little boy replied, "She's in the shower right now and can't come to the phone."

The salesman asked, "Well, is anyone else at home?"

"Yes," the boy said, "my sister is here."

"Well, okay," the salesman continued. "May I speak to her, please?"

"I guess so," the boy said. "I'll go get her."

At this point the salesman heard a clunk as the boy laid down the receiver. This was followed by a very long silence on the phone.

Finally the little boy came back on the line and said, "Are you still there?"

"Yes," the salesman answered, trying hard to sound patient, "I thought you were going to put your sister on the phone."

He replied, "I tried, mister. But she's sound asleep and I couldn't lift her out of her crib."

This humorous story aptly illustrates how concrete and innocent children are in their thinking. Which means, we are required to be clear in our expectations of and explanations to our children. We need to maintain our sense of humor, but never laugh at or ridicule them. This careful balance requires patience and *lots* of practice!

A merry heart doeth good like a medicine.

Proverbs 17:22

A sweater is a garment worn by a child when his mother feels chilly.

EIGHT-YEAR-OLD William was appreciative but not enthusiastic when he found skis under the Christmas tree. They had not been high on his wish list, but his mom and dad knew he would need them for an upcoming family trip.

As it turned out, the skis were the best gift he ever received. His first day on the slopes, William took to the sport and joined the resort's junior-racer program. For the next ten years, William skied every winter weekend, sometimes getting up in subzero cold to be at the mountain early. The skis taught him self-discipline and persistence. He learned to get up after falling hard. At home, he learned to budget his time to allow for homework. William became a hard-working, focused young adult willing to dare because he wasn't afraid to fail. The skis did for William what the long-gone record player and toy train could not.

Just as you give your children nutritious food to eat and make them wear warm clothing outside, choose your gifts wisely. Provide what is most beneficial, not necessarily what is desired. Give gifts that are challenging, bring out your children's talents, and broaden their creativity and horizons. Such gifts last far beyond one season!

She has no fear of winter for her household, for
she has made warm clothes for all of them.
 Proverbs 31:21 TLB

Any mother could perform the jobs of several air-traffic controllers with ease.

LILLIAN GILBRETH took an active role in Sunday school work. She didn't teach a class, but she served on a number of committees. Once she called on a woman who had just moved to town to ask her to serve on a fund-raising committee. "I'd be glad to if I had the time," the woman said, "but I have three young sons, and they keep me on the run. I'm sure if you have a boy of your own, you'll understand how much trouble three can be." Lillian replied, "Of course, that's quite all right. And I do understand."

"Have you any children, Mrs. Gilbreth?" the woman asked. Lillian replied, "Oh, yes." The woman pursued the line, "Any boys?" Lillian said, "Yes, indeed." The woman persisted, "May I ask how many?"

Lillian graciously replied, "Certainly. I have six boys."

The woman gulped, "Six boys? Imagine a family of six!" Lillian added, "Oh, there are more in the family than that. I have six girls, too."

As Frank B. Gilbreth Jr., and Ernestine Gilbreth Carey tell in their book, *Cheaper by the Dozen,* the newcomer then whispered, "I surrender. When is the next meeting of the committee? I'll be there, Mrs. Gilbreth. I'll be there."

How about you?

She looketh well to the ways of her household,
and eateth not the bread of idleness.
❧ Proverbs 31:27 ❧

*Parents must get across the idea that,
"I love you always, but I don't always
love your behavior."*

LITTLE Shannon misbehaved during dinner one evening. Her single mother, a strict but fair disciplinarian, reprimanded her. Still, Shannon didn't change her ways. The mother finally said, "Shannon, if you do not behave, you will be sent to your room, and there will be no more food for you tonight."

Shannon continued to misbehave. At that, she was ordered to march to her bedroom, change into her nightclothes, and climb into bed.

As she lay in bed, Shannon's every thought turned to food. She couldn't remember ever having felt hungrier or lonelier, or more alienated from the family. She began to cry. Then she heard a noise in the hallway and footsteps walking closer and closer to her room. The door opened and in came her mother.

Closing the door behind her, Shannon's mother sat down on the edge of the bed and brushed the tears from her daughter's eyes. "I love you, Shannon. Would you like me to read to you until you fall asleep?" Shannon snuffled and nodded "yes."

Not all behavior is worthy of applause. But every moment of a child's life and every ounce of a child's being is worthy of love. Look for ways to communicate this truth to your child today: "I always love you, but I don't always love your behavior."

Those whom I love, I reprove and discipline;
be zealous therefore, and repent.
— Revelation 3:19 NAS —

Level with your child by being honest.
Nobody spots a phony quicker than a child.

A LITTLE girl shouted with glee at the unexpected appearance of her grandmother in her nursery. "I've come to tuck you into bed and give you a goodnight kiss," the grandmother explained. "Will you read me a story first?" the little girl asked. Grandma, dressed elegantly for the impending dinner party downstairs, couldn't resist the soulful plea in her granddaughter's eyes. "All right," she replied, "but just one."

At the close of the story, the little girl snuggled into her bed, ready for sleep, but not before she said, "Thank you, Grandma. You look pretty tonight." The grandmother smiled and replied, "Yes, I have to be pretty for the dinner party your parents are hosting."

"I know," the little girl said. "Mommy and Daddy are entertaining some very important people downstairs."

"Why, yes," said the grandmother. "But how did you know that? Was it because I surprised you by coming upstairs tonight? Was it my dress that gave it away?" Each time her granddaughter shook her head "no." Finally, the grandmother asked, "Was it that I only read *one* story to you?"

"No," the little girl giggled. "Just listen! Mommy is laughing at all of Daddy's jokes."

Our kids catch on to much more than we realize. Be wise!

Pray for us: for we trust we have a good conscience, in all things willing to live honestly.

Hebrews 13:18

As parents, we never stand so tall as when we stoop to help our children.

IN her book, *American Girl,* Mary Cantwell tells of her great embarrassment and agony at not being able to do math like the other children in her class at school. She writes:

> It was agony to me to be so stupid. The more Miss Fritzi tried to show me how to translate the marks into symbols, the more cotton seemed to be stuffing the corners of my head. The cotton seemed even thicker on the nights Papa sat beside me at the desk in the living room, pencil points breaking under his fierce attack. . . . When at last my mother shyly volunteered, the suffering eyes we turned on her were identical.
>
> For several nights she sat at the desk . . . and summoned up her old schoolteacher's skills. Sniffling at her left, I bent over a scratch pad watching her small, shapely hand trace swoops and curlicues. Suddenly, they assembled themselves into sense and the cotton fled my head, leaving it as clear and clean as a tide-rinsed seashell. . . . I knew a triumph second only to that I'd known on the morning I finally succeeded in tying my shoelaces into bows. I could add!

Taking the time to help your children—no matter what the task—can change their world and yours.

Be humble, thinking of others as better than yourself. Don't just think about your own affairs, but be interested in others, too, and in what they are doing. Your attitude should be the kind that was shown us by Jesus Christ.

Philippians 2:3-5 TLB

*Children have more need of models
than of critics.*

THE daughter of missionaries to India, Wendy, resented being put into a "box" and as a teenager in boarding school, she rebelled against what was expected of her. Her parents returned to Canada so the family might be together, but Wendy continued to rebel. However, her mother and father didn't judge or condemn her. She says, "They just kept on loving me. I discovered that I could fight rules and people who criticized me, but I couldn't put up walls against love. Because of my parents' patient love for me, I stopped rebelling, and . . . I recommitted my life to Christ."

Wendy is now a missionary to India! One of her students, Anne, had a very negative attitude toward Christianity. Wendy said, "I prayed diligently for Anne and decided that I would treat her with the same lovingkindness with which my parents had treated me. I accepted Anne as she was, without placing spiritual expectations on her. When Anne realized that I didn't intend to judge her . . . she began opening up to me." In March, Anne accepted Christ into her life.

Wendy concludes, "A 'close family' has little to do with geography and being together physically. But [it] has everything to do with loving, supporting, and communicating with each other."

Be their ideal; let them follow the way you teach and live; be a pattern for them in your love, your faith, and your clean thoughts.
1 Timothy 4:12 TLB

*It is better to instill responsibility in
your children with kindness and
a sense of honor, rather than by fear.*

WHILE walking along a country road, a little girl found a land terrapin crawling across the warmed pavement. She moved closer to examine it, but the terrapin closed its shell like a vice. When she tried to pry it open with a stick, her mother intervened, "No, no. That is not the way. I'll show you what we need to do."

The mother picked up the small creature and carried it into the house. Then she set it on the hearth. In a few minutes, when the terrapin began to get warm, it stuck out its head and feet and calmly crawled toward the girl.

"People are sort of like terrapins, too," her mother said. "If you try to force people to do something, they'll usually close up tightly. But if you warm them up with a little kindness, they'll more than likely open up and come your way."

If you had to pick only one trait for a person you were expected to live around all the time, what would it be? Order, honor, bravery, knowledge, passion, fame? Probably not. The most desirable of all traits is the one every person can show: kindness. A kind word will turn aside anger and pour soothing words on a wound. Mix kindness with love, and you have the perfect combination!

Do not irritate and provoke your children to anger [do not exasperate them to resentment] but rear them [tenderly] in the training and discipline and the counsel and admonition of the Lord.
Ephesians 6:4 AMP

Encouragement is the art of motivating your children to do things for themselves rather than doing it for them.

ONCE upon a time there was a little boy who was given everything he wanted. As an infant, he was given a bottle at the first little whimper. He was picked up and held whenever he fussed. His parents said, "He'll think we don't love him if we let him cry."

He was never disciplined for leaving the yard, even after being told not to. He suffered no consequences for breaking windows or tearing up flower beds. His parents said, "He'll think we don't love him if we stifle his will."

His mother picked up after him and made his bed. His parents said, "He'll think we don't love him if we give him chores."

Nobody ever stopped him from using bad words. He was never reprimanded for scribbling on his bedroom wall. His parents said, "He'll think we don't love him if we stifle his creativity."

He never was required to go to Sunday school. His parents said, "He'll think we don't love him if we force religion down his throat."

One day the parents received news that their son was in jail on a felony charge. They cried to each other, "All we ever did was love him and do for him." Unfortunately, that is, indeed, *all* they did.

And thou shalt teach them ordinances and laws, and
shalt shew them the way wherein they must walk,
and the work that they must do.
Exodus 18:20

Home, sweet home—where each lives for the other, and all live for God.

IN *Secret Strength,* Joni Eareckson Tada writes a wonderful tribute to a genuine "home, sweet home":

> Not long ago I entered a friend's home and immediately sensed the glory of God. No, that impression was not based on some heebie-jeebie feeling or super-spiritual instinct. And it had nothing to do with several Christian plaques I spotted hanging in the hallway. Yet there was a peace and orderliness that pervaded that home. Joy and music hung in the air. Although the kids were normal, active youngsters, everyone's activity seemed to dovetail together, creating the impression that the home had direction, that the kids really cared about each other, that the parents put love into action.

> We didn't even spend that much time "fellowshipping" in the usual sense of the word— talking about the Bible or praying together. Yet we laughed. And really heard each other. And opened our hearts like family members. After dinner I left that home refreshed. It was a place where God's essential being was on display. His kindness, His love, His justice. It was filled with God's glory.

The presence of the Lord makes any home sweet. Invite Him into your home today.

For none of us lives to himself alone and none of us dies to himself alone. If we live, we live to the Lord; and if we die, we die to the Lord. So, whether we live or die, we belong to the Lord.

— Romans 14:7-8 NIV —

Children have never been very good at listening to their elders, but they have never failed to imitate them.

THE story is told of a devout Christian who was faithful in his daily devotions. He read portions of Scripture and a devotional book, meditated silently for awhile, and then prayed. As time went by, his prayers became longer and more intense. He came to cherish this quiet time in his bedroom. His cat liked it, too! She would snuggle against him, purring loudly. This interrupted the man, so he put a collar around the cat's neck and tied her to the bedpost whenever he wanted undisturbed devotional time.

The daughter of this man noticed how much his devotional time meant to him, and she adopted the practice. She dutifully tied her cat to the bedpost and proceeded to read and pray. Her prayer time was shorter, however. The day came when her son grew up. He desired also to keep some of the family traditions, but by his generation, the pace of life had quickened greatly. He felt he had no time for meditation, Bible reading, and prayer. Still, in order to carry on the religious tradition, while dressing each morning, he tied his cat to the bedpost!

Explain to your children why you keep certain rituals, lest they follow them blindly and they lose their meaning.

Ye know what manner of men we were among you for your sake. And ye became followers of us.
1 Thessalonians 1:5-6

Joy is the feeling of grinning inside.

Christmas Greetings.

TWO and a half years after artist Deneille Möes' mother became ill, she was finally diagnosed with Alzheimer's. As the disease progressed, Deneille watched as her mother's twenty-six grandchildren began to pull away from her, and even Deneille found herself withdrawing emotionally.

During the Christmas season following the diagnosis, Deneille just rushed through the motions of celebration. Knowing her mother didn't have much time left, she felt no joy in the carols, gift wrapping, and baking that usually filled her with great excitement.

After her mother died the following April, Deneille felt she would never enjoy another holiday season again. The next December, however, when she stepped out into the season's first snowfall—bright and white and filled with promise—joy flooded her heart. She had an inexplicable desire to celebrate the love of God and strength of family that her mother had embodied. Her brothers and sisters felt it, too, and the entire family decided to go home to be with Deneille's father for the holidays.

As she lay awake that Christmas Eve, Deneille felt the assurance of Psalm 30:5 KJV—"Weeping may endure for a night, but joy cometh in the morning."

Today, God desires for you to have His joy in your heart!

For you shall go out with joy, and be led out with peace.
Isaiah 55:12 NKJV

A mother . . . fills a place so great that there isn't an angel in heaven who wouldn't be glad to give a bushel of diamonds to come down here and take her place.

A THIRTEEN-YEAR-OLD girl named Amy was not only struggling with growing into womanhood, but also with discovering her "identity." She had been adopted from South Korea and had no information about or remembrance of her birth mother. As much as she loved her adoptive parents, she began to speak frequently about what her "real mother" might be like.

During this time, Amy's dentist determined that Amy needed braces. On the day her braces were fitted, Amy went home from the dentist's office in pain. As the day wore on, her discomfort grew; and by bedtime, she was miserable. Her mother gave her medication and then invited her to snuggle up in her lap in the rocking chair, just as she had done when she was a little girl. As the mother rocked and stroked Amy's hair, she began to relax. She was nearly asleep when she said to her mother in a drowsy voice, "I know who my real mom is."

"You do?" her mother asked gently.

"Yes," she replied. "She's the one who takes away the hurting."

Mothers may not always be able to "kiss it and make it better," but the love they give their children goes a long way toward making their children whole.

And the angel came in unto her, and said, Hail,
thou that art highly favoured, the Lord is with thee:
blessed art thou among women.

Luke 1:28

A mother is the one who is still there when everyone else has deserted you.

A NUMBER of years ago a popular Mother's Day card summed up what many adult women feel. The cover of the card read, "Now that we have a mature, adult relationship, there's something I'd like to tell you." On the inside were these words: "You're still the first person I think of when I fall down and go boom."

None of us ever get beyond feeling a need for our mothers—the one person who has nurtured us, comforted us, and cared for us as no other person ever has or ever will. It is only when we are mothers ourselves, however, that we tend to realize how important our own mothers were to us.

As Victoria Farnsworth has written:

Not until I became a mother did I understand
　　How much my mother had sacrificed for me.
Not until I became a mother did I feel
　　How hurt my mother was when I disobeyed.
Not until I became a mother did I know
　　How proud my mother was when I achieved.
Not until I became a mother did I realize
　　How much my mother loves me.

Therefore, be encouraged. One day, your children will feel the same way.

If you love someone you will be loyal to him
no matter what the cost.
1 Corinthians 13:7 TLB

*The best way to cheer yourself up is
to cheer up somebody else.*

THE grief-stricken mother sat in a hospital room in stunned silence, tears streaming down her cheeks. She had just lost her only child. She gazed into space as the head nurse asked her, "Did you notice the little boy sitting in the hall just outside?" The woman shook her head "no."

The nurse continued. "His mother was brought here by ambulance from their poor one-room apartment. The two of them came to this country only three months ago, because all their family members had been killed in war. They don't know anyone here.

"That little boy has been sitting outside his mother's room every day for a week in hopes his mother would come out of her coma and speak to him."

By now the woman was listening intently as the nurse continued, "Fifteen minutes ago, his mother died. It's my job to tell him that, at age seven, he is all alone in the world—there's nobody who even knows his name." The nurse paused and then asked, "I don't suppose you would tell him for me?" The woman stood, dried her tears, and went out to the boy.

She put her arms around the homeless child. She invited him to come with her to her childless home. In the darkest hour of both their lives, they became lights to each other.

Give, and it shall be given unto you.

Luke 6:38

When Mother Teresa received her
Nobel Prize, she was asked,
"What can we do to promote world peace?"
She replied, "Go home and love your family."

A MOTHER'S letters to her son, Johannes, give a strong impression of her clear common sense and her great kindheartedness. She reports all the interesting news from Hamburg, never speaking ill of anyone. When his brother, Fritz, lost an excellent job, she wrote to Johannes: "Fritz must put his trust in God, who guides all human destinies. He will lead him out of this darkness." She remembered Johannes daily in her prayers, as well as Elise and Fritz, and tried to keep a tight bond among her children, reminding Johannes to remember their birthdays. There is no sign in her letters of any disharmony in her marriage, which lasted thirty-four years; and generally speaking, peace and cheerfulness seemed to prevail in her household.

In sharp contrast was the world outside their home: a poverty-stricken slum with narrow, crooked streets and grime-encrusted, "blackened" frame houses. Disease was rampant, and if fire broke out, the effects on the neighborhood were devastating.

What was the impact of this mother's nurturing goodness on her son? Through the centuries, the compelling, beautiful music of Johannes Brahms has touched countless millions.

Your daily example of love and kindness is written upon the hearts of your children. Inscribe wisdom on the delicate pages of their souls.

Let love and faithfulness never leave you; bind them around your neck, write them on the tablet of your heart.

Proverbs 3:3 NIV

When people ask me what I do,
I always say I am a mother first.

POPULAR writer and speaker Tony Campolo tells this story about his wife. When he was on the faculty of the University of Pennsylvania, his wife was often invited to faculty gatherings, and inevitably a woman lawyer or sociologist would confront her with the question, often framed in a condescending tone of voice, "And what is it that you do, my dear?"

Mrs. Campolo gave this as her response: "I am socializing two Homo sapiens in the dominant values of the Judeo-Christian tradition in order that they might be instruments for the transformation of the social order into the theologically prescribed utopia inherent in the eschaton." Then she would politely and kindly ask the other person, "And what is it that you do?"

The other person's response was rarely as overpowering!

Too often, women feel as if they should apologize for being mothers or wives who "work at home" for the betterment of their families and husbands. In reality, these roles can be noble callings—ones with far-reaching impact and eternal consequences! Don't ever apologize for being "just a housewife." Remember the job description given by Mrs. Campolo. You are valuable. You are making a tremendous contribution to society. Don't forget it!

Many women do noble things, but you surpass them all.
— Proverbs 31:29 NIV —

Encouraging your children to become unique, productive individuals is a more worthy occupation than hanging around with supposedly important people.

A LITTLE girl, only three years old, had just learned she was adopted, but she had not reacted in one way or the other to the news. Her mother was at a loss as to how to explain the adoption any further.

The next day at church, the little girl watched as a number of people came forward at the close of the service to accept Jesus Christ as their Savior and Lord. She asked her mother, "What are they doing?" Her mother was quick to reply, "God has offered to adopt them all as His children, and they are taking Him up on His offer so they can live with Him forever in heaven and always know that He loves them with all His heart." The little girl nodded and watched in awe as the pastor prayed with each person.

The next day, the mother overheard her little girl speak into her cocker spaniel's ear, "I just wanted you to know I'm 'dopting you 'cause God and Mommy and Daddy have 'dopted me. And that way we can live together forever."

Never assume that a child is too young to follow Christ. Regardless of age, encourage your child to make that choice.

The fruit of the righteous is a tree of life;
and he that winneth souls is wise.
Proverbs 11:30

A mother's patience is like a tube of toothpaste—
it's never quite gone.

ACCORDING to a fable, a woman showed up one snowy morning at 5 a.m. at the home of an "examiner" of "suitable mother" candidates. Ushered in, she was asked to sit for three hours past her appointment time before she was interviewed. The first question given to her in the interview was, "Can you spell?"

"Yes," she said. "Then spell 'cook.'" The woman responded, "C-O-O-K."

The examiner than asked, "Do you know anything about numbers?" The woman replied, "Yes, sir, some things." The examiner said, "Please add two plus two." The candidate replied, "Four."

"Fine," announced the examiner. "We'll be in touch." At the board meeting of examiners held the next day, the examiner reported that the woman had all the qualifications to be a fine mother. He said, "First I tested her on self-denial, making her arrive at five in the morning on a snowy day. Then I tested her on patience. She waited three hours without complaint. Third, I tested her on temper, asking her questions a child could answer. She never showed indignation or anger. She'll make a fine mother." And all on the board agreed.

When you think you've run out of patience, remember the toothpaste tube—just squeeze a little harder!

Being strengthened with all power according to his glorious might so that you may have great endurance and patience.

✎ Colossians 1:11 NIV ✐

The school will teach children how to read, but the environment of the home must teach them what to read. The school can teach them how to think, but the home must teach them what to believe.

LEWIS SMEDES of Fuller Theological Seminary, has written a wonderful tribute to the impact a godly home can have upon a child's faith:

May I share with you some reasons why I believe? . . . There's my family. I believe because I was brought up in a believing family. I don't make any bones about that. I don't know what would have happened to me if I had been born in the depths of Manchuria of a Chinese family. I just don't know. I do know that I was led to believe in the love of God as soon as I learned I should eat my oatmeal. We did a lot of believing in our house. . . . Other kids sang, "Jesus loves me this I know 'cause the Bible tells me so." I sang, "Jesus loves me this I know, 'cause my ma told me so."

I wasn't alone. You probably heard about a reporter asking the great German theologian, Karl Barth, toward the end of his career: "Sir, you've written these great volumes about God, great learned tomes about all the difficult problems of God. How do you know they're all true?" And the great theologian smiled and said, "'Cause my mother said so!"

Families are God's primary missionary society.

Teach a child to choose the right path, and when he is older he will remain upon it.
 Proverbs 22:6 TLB

Kind words can be short and easy to speak,
but their echoes are truly endless.

KINDNESS provides a house, but love makes a home.

Kindness packs an adequate sack lunch, but love puts a note of encouragement inside.

Kindness provides a television set or computer as a learning aid, but love controls the remote control and cares enough to insist a child "sign off."

Kindness sends a child to bed on time, but love tucks the covers around a child's neck and provides a goodnight hug and kiss.

Kindness cooks a meal, but love selects the "your favorite foods" menu and lights the candles.

Kindness writes a thank-you note, but love thinks to include a joke or photograph or bookmark inside the envelope.

Kindness keeps a clean and tidy house, but love adds a bouquet of fresh flowers.

Kindness pours a glass of milk, but love occasionally adds a little chocolate sauce.

Kindness is doing what is decent, basic, courteous, and necessary for an even, smooth, and gentle flow of life.

Love is taking the extra step to make life truly exciting, creative, and meaningful!

A mother's love is what makes things *special!*

She opens her mouth in skillful and godly Wisdom, and on her tongue is the law of kindness [giving counsel and instruction].

Proverbs 31:26 AMP

God has given you your child, that the sight of him (or her), from time to time, might remind you of His goodness, and induce you to praise Him with filial reverence.

WHILE driving along a freeway on a cold, rainy night, the adults in the front seat of a car were talking when suddenly, they heard the horrifying sound of a car door opening, then the whistle of wind, and a sickening muffled sound. They quickly turned and saw that the three-year-old child riding in the backseat had fallen out of the car and was tumbling along the freeway. The driver screeched to a stop, and then raced back toward her motionless child. To her surprise, she found all the traffic had stopped just feet away from her child. Her daughter had not been hit.

A truck driver offered his assistance and drove the girl to a nearby hospital. The doctors rushed her into the emergency room, and soon came back with the good news: Other than being unconscious, bruised, and skinned up from her tumble, the girl was fine.

As the mother rushed to her child, the little girl opened her eyes and said, "Mommy, I wasn't scared." The mother asked, "What do you mean?" The little girl explained, "While I was lying on the road waiting for you to come get me, I looked up and right there I saw Jesus holding back the cars."

Even when we are distracted and neglect our children on occasion, God is still on duty, watching over them.

See how very much our heavenly Father loves us, for he allows us to be called his children—think of it—and we really are!

☙ 1 John 3:1 TLB ❧

Your children learn more of your faith
during the bad times than they do
during the good times.

WHEN Eleanor Sass was a child, she was hospitalized for appendicitis. Her roommate was a young girl named Mollie, who was injured when an automobile hit the bicycle she was riding. Mollie's legs had been badly broken, and although the doctors had performed several surgeries, Mollie faced the strong possibility that she would never walk again. She became depressed and uncooperative. She only seemed to perk up when the morning mail arrived. Most of her gifts were books, games, and stuffed animals—all appropriate gifts for a bedridden child.

Then one day a different sort of gift came, this one from an aunt far away. When Mollie tore open the package, she found a pair of shiny, black-patent-leather shoes. The nurses in the room mumbled something about "people who don't use their heads," but Mollie didn't seem to hear them. She was too busy putting her hands in the shoes and "walking" them up and down her blanket. From that day forward, her attitude changed. She began cooperating with the nursing staff, and soon, she was in therapy. One day Eleanor heard that her friend had left the hospital . . . and the best news of all, she had walked out, wearing her shiny new shoes!

Teach your children that faith believes the impossible!

Consider it all joy, my brethren, when you encounter various trials.
James 1:2 NAS

A woman who can cope with the "terrible twos" can cope with anything.

DURING a dinner party, the hosts' two young children suddenly entered the dining room totally nude and began to slowly tiptoe around the table. The parents were at first so astonished, and then so embarrassed, that they pretended nothing unusual was happening. They kept the conversation going, and the guests cooperated in the charade, also pretending nothing extraordinary was happening in the room.

After completely encircling the table, the children tiptoed from the room. There was a moment of silence at the table as everyone exhaled and stifled their giggles. Then one of the children was overheard saying to the other in the adjacent hallway, "You see, Mommy was right. It is vanishing cream!"

While their rambunctious energy and inexhaustible curiosity can be tiring to adults, toddlers don't mean to misbehave nearly as much as they mean to make sense of the world in which they find themselves. Your discipline, patience, and encouragement are like red, yellow, and green lights governing their expedition through the exploration process.

When your children try your patience, remember that the "terrible twos" will be over before you know it, and in the end, you'll have some great storytelling material!

The LORD is on my side; I will not fear:
what can man do unto me?
Psalm 118:6

Parenthood is a partnership with God . . . you are working with the Creator of the universe in shaping human character and determining destiny.

OH, heavenly Father, make me a better parent. Teach me to understand my children, to listen patiently to what they have to say, and to answer all their questions kindly. Keep me from interrupting them or contradicting them. Make me as courteous to them as I would have them be to me. Forbid that I should ever laugh at their mistakes, or resort to shame or ridicule when they displease me. May I never punish them for my own selfish satisfaction.

Let me not tempt my child to lie or steal. And guide me hour by hour that I may demonstrate by all I say and do that honesty produces happiness. And when I am out of sorts, help me, Oh Lord, to hold my tongue. May I ever be mindful that my children are children and I should not expect of them the judgment of adults.

Let me not rob them of the opportunity to wait on themselves and to make decisions. Bless me with the bigness to give them all their reasonable requests, and the courage to deny them privileges I know will do them harm. . . . And fit me, Oh Lord, to be loved and respected and imitated by my children. Amen.

—Abigail Van Buren

We are labourers together with God.

1 Corinthians 3:9

Small boy: "If I'm noisy they give me a spanking . . . and if I'm quiet they take my temperature."

KAIS RAYES writes that he and his wife found their whole life turned upside down when their first child was born. Every night, the baby seemed to be fussy, and many nights, it seemed to the young couple that their baby cried far more than he slept. Says Rayes, "My wife would wake me up, saying, 'Get up, honey! Go see why the baby is crying!'" As a result, Rayes found himself suffering from severe sleep deprivation.

One day while complaining to his co-workers about his problem, one of his colleagues suggested a book on infant massage. He immediately went in search of the book; and that night, he tried the technique, gently rubbing his baby's back, arms, head, and legs until the baby was completely relaxed and obviously had fallen into a deep sleep. Quietly tiptoeing from the darkened room so as not to disturb the rhythmic breathing of the baby, he made his way directly to his own bed in hopes of enjoying a well-deserved night of uninterrupted sleep.

But in the middle of the night, his wife awoke him in a panic. "Get up, honey!" she said as she jostled him awake. "Go see why the baby is *not* crying!"

A merry heart doeth good like a medicine.
 Proverbs 17:22

Who ran to me when I fell, and would some pretty story tell, or kiss the place to make it well? My mother.

A YOUNG girl was late in coming home from school. Her mother watched the clock nervously and with growing concern. Finally she arrived. Her mother, nearly frantic at that point, hugged her daughter, and after giving her a thorough appraisal and realizing nothing appeared to be wrong, demanded, "Where were you? What took you so long? Haven't I told you to be home by four o'clock?"

The girl answered her mother's first question, "I was at Mary's house."

"And what was so important that you couldn't get home on time?" her mother scolded.

Her daughter replied, "Her favorite doll got broken."

"Did you break it?" the mother asked. When her daughter shook her head "no," she then asked, "Could the doll be fixed?" Again, the girl replied, "No." Both bewildered and frustrated, the mother asked a third time, "So what was the point of staying so long?"

Tears began to well up in the little girl's eyes and stream down her face under her mother's inquisition.

"I helped her cry," she said softly.

The Scriptures tell us to *rejoice with them that do rejoice, and weep with them that weep* (Romans 12:15). A mother may not be able to do everything for her children, but we all can do that!

As one whom his mother comforteth, so will I comfort you.

🙟 Isaiah 66:13 🙞

Remember, when your child has a tantrum,
don't have one of your own.

A MOTHER was at her wit's end. Her baby had screamed all day, nonstop. She knew he was in the throes of teething, but what could she do? She had tried everything. Finally, in great frustration, she laid her child in his crib, took a shower, washed her hair, set it, and went to sit under her hair dryer. She thought, *If I can't stop my baby's crying, at least I can stop myself from hearing his cries.*

To her surprise, when she came out from under the hair dryer to get a drink of water, she found her baby asleep. The next day when he began to cry, she turned on the hair dryer, and within minutes, he was calm. She discovered the vacuum cleaner also had this effect, as well as the sound of the tumbling dryer. She said, "I got more housework done than I ever dreamed possible, all in an attempt to calm my child."

Sometimes tantrums are the result of over-stimulation. A child is too tired, surrounded by too many sights and sounds, feeling too many conflicting feelings, and even receiving too much reaction from parents! In removing some of the stimulation, a child is given just what he or she needs—calm.

And every man that striveth for the
mastery is temperate in all things.
1 Corinthians 9:25

The only thing children wear out faster than shoes are parents and teachers.

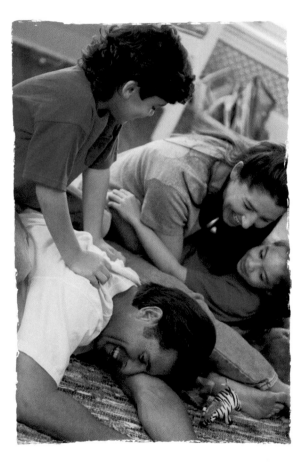

IN her book, *Murphy Must Have Been a Mother,* Teresa Bloomingdale tells about her daughter's preparing for high school. "I don't have anything to wear," the daughter complained.

Mother agreed, "I know that, honey, and I told you we'd go on a shopping spree next Saturday."

"I can't buy clothes now!" the daughter said.

"Why not? School starts next week," asked Mom.

The daughter said, "I can't get clothes for school until I go to school and see what clothes I should get. What if I showed up in jeans and all the other girls were in skirts? I'd die!"

"Then wear a skirt," the mother suggested.

"And find everyone else in jeans?" When Mom suggested she call a friend and find out what she was going to wear, the daughter said, "Are you kidding? She'd think I don't have a mind of my own!"

Another friend finally called and the two girls decided on their first-day-of-the-year outfits: blue jeans, white knit shirts, white bobby sox, and topsider shoes. The author wrote, "and these are the girls who spent eight years complaining because they had to wear look-alike uniforms!"

When you can't understand the logic of a teenage daughter, remember you were once a teenage girl too. Then, you'll understand!

He gives power to the tired and worn out,
and strength to the weak.
Isaiah 40:29 TLB

A little boy, age eight, gave a profound definition of parenthood: "Parents are just baby-sitters for God."

A WOMAN was preparing to leave her child with a baby-sitter while she joined her husband for the weekend. Since her husband had been out of town for several weeks she was looking forward to their time together, although she was experiencing a little fear and doubt about leaving her four-year-old daughter at home. She watched from a window as her daughter churned down the driveway on her tricycle, making a sharp right turn at the tree. Her "driving" over the tree roots, however, ended in the tricycle tipping over. Wailing, she came running into the house and lifted her skinned knee for her mother to kiss it.

"Who will kiss my knee while you're away?" her daughter asked, her chin quivering. The mother was about to mention the baby-sitter when she heard herself saying, "I know! God will do it." Her daughter beamed, well satisfied with that answer, and immediately headed back to her tricycle.

The mother found her answer reviving her own faith, and she left for her weekend feeling much more positive about leaving her daughter in the Heavenly Father's hands!

It's helpful to daily remind yourself that your children ultimately belong to God. Make it a practice to daily give your children to Him.

I prayed for this child, and the LORD has granted me what I asked of him. So now I give him to the LORD. For his whole life he will be given over to the LORD.

1 Samuel 1:27-28 NIV

*My mother was the source from which
I derived the guiding principles of my life.*

DURING a special program at church, a little girl was to recite the Scripture she had been assigned for the occasion. When she got in front of the crowd, however, the sight of hundreds of eyes peering at her caused her to have a bout of stage fright. She completely forgot her verse and was unable to utter a single word.

Her mother, sitting in the front row, leaned forward, and after several attempts, finally got her daughter's attention. She moved her lips and gestured but her daughter didn't seem to comprehend what she was doing. Finally the mother whispered the opening phrase of the verse she was to recite, "I am the light of the world."

The little girl's face lit up and she smiled with confidence. "My mother is the light of the world!" she announced boldly.

Her words brought a smile to the face of each audience member, and yet upon reflection, most had to admit that she had declared an eloquent truth. A mother is the light of her child's world.

Let your light shine brightly today on your child's behalf!

Be ye followers of me, even as I also am of Christ.

1 Corinthians 11:1

Acknowledgments

WE acknowledge and thank the following people for the quotes used in this book: C. H. Spurgeon (6), Ruth Bell Graham (8), Thomas Fessenden (12), Madeline Cox (14), V. Gilbert Beers (16), Henry Ward Beecher (20,80), Penelope Leach (22), Imogene Fey (24), James Dobson (26,66), Wilfred A. Peterson (28,38), Mary Cholmondeley (30), Earl Riney (34), Dr. Anthony P. Witham (36,90,154), Lowell (40), Erma Bombeck (42), Mary Lamb (44), Henry Ward Beecher (46), Jean Hodges (48), *Milwaukee Journal* (50), T. L. Cuyler (54), Abraham Lincoln (56,100), Henry Wadsworth Longfellow (60), Leo J. Burke (62), Lin Yutang (64), Henry Home (68), Ed Dussault (70), Lionel M. Kaufman (76), Lady Bird Johnson (78), Shannon Fife (82), Mildred B. Vermont (84), Peter Marshall (94), Oliver Wendell Holmes (96), *Reader's Digest* (97), Barbara Bush (98), Lane Olinhouse (102), Helen Steiner Rice (104), Dr. William Mitchell and Dr. Charles Paul Conn (106,160), G. W. C. Thomas (108), Pope Paul VI (110), Katherine Whitehouse (112), Mary Howitt (114), James Keller (116), Renee Jordan (118), Theresa Ann Hunt (120), Larry Christenson (128), Alvin Vander Griend (130), Leo Tolstoy (132), Betty Mills (134), Phyllis Diller (136), Sir P. Sidney (138), John Lobbock (140), Barbara Johnson (146), Lisa Alther (148), Amy Vanderbilt (150), M. MacCracken (152), Joseph Joubert (156), Terence (158), T. J. Bach (162), James Baldwin (164), Carl Sandburg (166), *Guideposts* (167), Billy Sunday (168), St. Basil (172), David Wilkerson (174), Jacqueline Jackson (176), John Hay (178), Charles A. Wells (182), Mother Teresa (184), Christian Scriver (186), Beverly LaHaye (188), Judy Clabes (190), Ruth Vaughn (192), Coronet (194), Ann Taylor (196), Dr. J. Kuriansky (198), John Wesley (204).